MODERN
LANGUAGE
ASSOCIATION

MLA style is about to get easier for writers and teachers

MLA Handbook
9th edition

FORTHCOMING APRIL 2021

Visit style.mla.org to learn more.

**Rhetoric &
Composition**
PhD Program

PROGRAM
Pioneering program honoring the rhetorical tradition through scholarly innovation, excellent job placement record, well-endowed library, state-of-the-art New Media Writing Studio, and graduate certificates in new media and women's studies.

TEACHING
1-1 teaching loads, small classes, extensive pedagogy and technology training, and administrative fellowships in writing program administration and new media.

FACULTY
Nationally recognized teacher-scholars in history of rhetoric, modern rhetoric, women's rhetoric, digital rhetoric, composition studies, and writing program administration.

FUNDING
Generous four-year graduate instructorships, competitive stipends, travel support, and several prestigious fellowship opportunities.

EXPERIENCE
Mid-sized liberal arts university setting nestled in the vibrant, culturally-rich Dallas-Fort Worth metroplex.

English
DEPARTMENT
Contact Dr. Mona Narain
m.narain@tcu.edu
eng.tcu.edu

composition
STUDIES

Volume 48, Number 3

Fall 2020

SUBSCRIPTIONS

Composition Studies is published twice each year (May and November). Annual subscription rates: Individuals $25 (Domestic), $30 (International), and $15 (Students). To subscribe on-line, please visit https://compstudiesjournal.com/subscriptions/.

BACK ISSUES

Back issues, five years prior to the present, are freely accessible on our website: https://comp studiesjournal.com/archive/. If you don't see what you're looking for, contact us. Also, recent back issues are now available through Amazon.com. To find issues, use the advanced search feature and search on "Composition Studies" (title) and "Parlor Press" (publisher).

BOOK REVIEWS

Assignments are made from a file of potential book reviewers. If you are interested in writing a review, please contact our Book Review editor at Jason.Tham@ttu.edu.

JOURNAL SCOPE

The oldest independent periodical in the field, *Composition Studies* publishes original articles relevant to rhetoric and composition, including those that address teaching college writing; theorizing rhetoric and composing; administering writing programs; and, among other topics, preparing the field's future teacher-scholars. All perspectives and topics of general interest to the profession are welcome. We also publish Course Designs, which contextualize, theorize, and reflect on the content and pedagogy of a course. CFPs, announcements, and letters to the editor are most welcome. *Composition Studies* does not consider previously published manuscripts, unrevised conference papers, or unrevised dissertation chapters.

SUBMISSIONS

For submission information and guidelines, see https://compstudiesjournal.com/submissions/.

Direct all correspondence to:

Matthew Davis, Co-Editor
Department of English
UMass Boston
100 Morrissey Blvd
Boston MA 02125–3393
compstudiesjournal@gmail.com

Composition Studies is grateful for the support of the University of Massachusetts Boston and the University of Denver.

© 2020 by Matthew Davis and Kara Taczak, Co-Editors

Production and distribution is managed by Parlor Press, www.parlorpress.com.

ISSN 1534–9322.

Cover art by Tig May.

https://compstudiesjournal.com/

composition STUDIES

Volume 48, Number 3

Fall 2020

Contents

Book Reviews

From the Editors: Checking In

Are you ok?

2020 has been a long year.

When we last wrote, COVID-19 had the country—indeed the globe—on late spring lockdown. Since then, the total COVID-19 deaths in the United States has reached over 230,000. The total deaths worldwide are now over 1.25 million. Over the summer, fires raged in the American West, hurricanes battered the Gulf states, and an economic depression set in from coast to coast. At the same time, peaceful social justice protests across the country were met with violence—from counter protesters and police alike—as one of the most bitter, divisive presidential campaigns in recent memory played out across screens, platforms, and geographies. The daily barrage of violence, oppression, mendacity, and unnecessary suffering was, it seemed, more than America could bear. And that was just in the United States.

In our little corner of the world, it often felt like more than teachers could bear, too. Multiple new teaching models emerged—remote, flex, hyflex—each compounding the work of teaching and the exposure of teachers and students more than the last. In some cases, schools began and stayed remote. Others opened, then closed. Still others closed, then reopened, and even now some institutions are moving online after months of being open. The results have been harrowing for higher education teachers and students alike. (This is especially true for those who teach and learn at multiple institutions with differing responses to the crisis). Similarly, academic research has been disrupted across the country. Researchers have had to pause programs and studies, give away precious, guarded writing time, and even fight against retrenchment of the humanities faculty at their institutions. Administrators—often also teachers and researchers—have had to move programs online at a moment's notice, often with no support, no compensation, and no stable institutional response from which to work. For many, this was lonely work: working from home meant missing supportive campus communities, the satisfaction of face-to-face collaboration with colleagues, and the esprit de corps of working with students. For others, this work was far too social: living rooms, kitchens, and bedrooms turned into makeshift offices so that children and partners could continue their work from home as well. For still others, it meant no work at all: the disappearance of guaranteed teaching sections, of needed income, of spaces for institutional and disciplinary belonging.

And, as is too often the case in this country, the suffering was born unequally: women and people of color were disproportionately affected by the virus, the devastation, the shifts; it was an inordinate amount of their work required to try and make things right again.

Just now, however, more Americans came together—despite their differences—to vote and thereby to shape the next era of government. Perhaps, we've set a new stage for Americans to listen to each other more and to work together to bridge the social, cultural, professional, racial, and gender inequities that have been exasperated by the pandemic. We look forward to playing our small role in that brighter future.

It was a long year for the world, for the country, for teachers, researchers, and admins, for students, and a long year for us.

So we're writing to check in on you. We *do* hope you are well. We hope your loved ones are well. We hope that your students and colleagues are well. And we hope you will stay well.

Here at the journal, we are well.

We are also growing. This year, we've added a number of new members to the *Composition Studies* team (and promoted others!). Our masthead, starting in spring 2021, will include:

- Megan Busch (South Carolina), as managing editor;
- Lauren Fusilier (Louisville) and Megan van Bergen (UT Knoxville) as blog editors;
- Mike Haen (Wisconsin-Madison), Callie Kostelich (Texas Tech), Emma Kostopoulos (U of Kansas), Alex McAdams (Rice), and Clare Sully-Stendahl (U of King's College) as content and revision editors; and
- Nitya Pandey (Florida State) and Annemarie Steffes (St. Francis) as social media editors.

We feel humbled to welcome these talented folks to the journal, and we're confident that *CS* readers will benefit immensely from their skill, dedication, and energy. Our trusted editorial assistant, Wafaa Razeq, will be graduating with her MA from UMass Boston (congrats!) and moving on to a graduate program in library science. We are grateful for her diligent and thorough work, and we wish her all the best in the future.

Additionally, we are thrilled to announce plans for the publication of another open-access, digital special issue in summer 2021. This issue, guest co-edited by Ersula Ore, Kim Wieser, and Christina Cedillo, builds on their work around diversity and justice upcoming in other venues by focusing on the perspectives of BIPOC faculty with respect to disciplinary and institutional exclusionary practices. In summer 2021, the issue will be released fully online on our website. We are also seeking collaborative editorial teams for summer 2022, so if you have a possible topic, please submit a proposal to <compstudiesjournal@gmail.com>

This Issue

The practice of vibrant, creative cover art at *CS* continues. For the fall 2020 issue, Dr. Talitha May created this stark and lively cover. To accompany the composition, Talitha writes:

> The woven ecology/social fabric of intersections and repetitions in the cover art meditates on our collective moment. With worldwide Covid-19 deaths in the hundreds of thousands, the flowers take on the role of funeral flowers and invite us to take pause and grieve. The art also draws attention to wicked problems. The landscape suggests that woven throughout our institutions, racism intersects with oppressive systems sustaining inequality. The crowded composition reminds viewers that individuals are complicit in systemic racism—no outside positionality exists. Nonetheless, the open canvas suggests we can create alternative futures.

We find this piece evocative of both our present difficulties and the energy and beauty of a future toward which we can collectively strive. We're grateful to Talitha for lending her art to our cover.

At A Glance: Connections and Collaborations

Always thoughtful, provocative, and probing, Asao Inoue and Mya Poe, well known for their work—individually and collaboratively—on anti-racist writing assessment, created the At A Glance infographic for this issue. This is a compelling contribution: first, because it outlines a number of questions that teachers and administrators can ask themselves when striving towards anti-racism in the classroom and in programmatic initiatives; second, because it is framed as a helpful framework for faculty development more generally; and third, because the infographic is accompanied by a wonderful handout and bibliography, both of which will appear on the *CS* website at <https://comp-studiesjournal.com/current-issue—fall-2020-48-3/>

The Articles

The slate of articles in this issue is fitting for our current moment: they cluster, serendipitously, around the theme of *better ways of working together*. Jennifer Ansley's article continues a disciplinary discussion about rethinking archives, how to work in them, and how to teach about them from a queer perspective. By thinking and teaching archives queerly, Ansley not only opens space for investigating archives of queer communities but also for queer ways of investigating archival communities. The result of her framework is that teachers and students approach archives by holding in tension the desire to make sense of archives and the kind of self-conscious reflection on positionality, narrative, and ethics that knowledge production—and perhaps queerness itself—requires.

Rachel McCabe and Elizabeth Maffetone chronicle how unexpected collaboration—which they term "inventive collaboration"—can emerge from well articulated training programs and, when facilitated by institutional-ecological thinking, can promote student success in writing. With one as instructor and one as writing center specialist, McCabe and Maffetone engage in a kind of collaboration-by-proxy, centered on student writing, that results in a stronger bonds among disparate campus entities, an innovative model for supporting student writers, and evidence of improved agency on the part of the student writer with whom they work.

Finally, Debra Dimond Young and Rachel Morgan provide a study of student writers asking how the combination of community-engaged courses and rhetorically-attuned pedagogy influences student writing processes. In studying 4 sections of a first year communication course, Young and Morgan find three important impacts of "writing for the community" (Deans) that will be of interest to researchers of student writing: changes in students' conceptions of writing itself; adjustments in the strategies students use for specific audiences; and, based on that, reconfiguration of students' revision practices.

The Course Designs

This issue offers three course designs, all very different from one to the next. First, Ashanka Kumari and Brita M. Thielen share a unit for an introductory writing course focused on engaging identities, cultivating compassion, and modeling vulnerability: all outcomes of the way in which they—and their students—discuss privilege as a way to link their personal identities to larger systems of opportunity and oppression. Next, weaving their course revision to the threads of programmatic, collegiate, and university expectations, Laura Hardin Marshall and Paul Lynch show how they see the introductory writing course as a laboratory (or a place where thinking happens), not a space oriented to the delivery of written products. This allows teachers and students to engage rhetorical challenges both ancient and contemporary. Finally, Vanessa Cozza's design outlines how to productively integrate client-based projects (or CBPs) into upper-level technical and professional writing courses. Cozza's course serves as a model for coordinating internal (at the university) and external (in the community) opportunities to serve as adaptable, immersive learning and writing experiences for students.

The Where We Are Section

This issue's Where We Are focuses on something we've all encountered plenty in 2020: bullshit. Starting from—and then pushing past—Harry Frankfurt's important 2005 work, *On Bullshit*, this section offers perspectives on seeing bullshit as an epistemic, identity-informed, discursive formation with implications for personal and public rhetoric, ethics, politics, as well as the classroom. The pieces, each in their own way, strive to both understand and study bullshit and, in doing so, they are ungirded by a shared commitment to intersubjective reality and the role of language in shaping our understanding of and engagement with it.

The Book Reviews

The book reviews begin with Christina V. Cedillo's powerful review essay on (inter-)cultural literacies in which she pushes instructors to be more aware how they uphold white supremacist values. To counter white supremacy, Cedillo draws on Inoue to urge instructors toward "'deep listening' that deprioritizes [their] own habituated expectations and allows others to speak for themselves" (Inoue 363). Within the context of linguistic and racialized violence, Cedillo's review captures how these two works provide paths for "interrupt[ing] white language supremacy's violent designs."

Next, Jamie White-Farnham's focused review essay tracks an uptick in composition scholarship on ethics through two linked projects with shared subtitles that make their contribution clear: "Rhetoric, Ethics, and the Teaching of Writing." White-Farnham's review outlines how these books push past traditional touchstones for ethics and virtue—moving from the "Q Question" (Quintilian, of course!) and toward the "P Question," (possibilities, naturally). This move, White-Farnham argues, orients attention away from specific theorists of ethics and virtue and toward "a more persuasive and workable … both/and" approach to engaging with Western and non-Western rhetorical traditions.

We also have four exciting reviews focused on various aspects of the classroom: digital archives, translingual realities, rhetorical empathy, and paragraphs.

As 2020 slowly winds down and courses wrap up and the last remaining grades are calculated, we're hopeful that brighter days await us all.

In closing, we invite you to answer our opening question, if you're so inclined, in our social media spaces—Facebook, Twitter, or Instagram. We genuinely would love to hear and share in the good and the not-so-good; at *CS*, we believe in listening and learning from each other's moments of hurt and triumph.

MD and Kt
Boston and Denver
November 2020

How to Stop Harming Students: An Ecological Guide to Antiracist Writing Assessment

Asao B. Inoue with Mya Poe

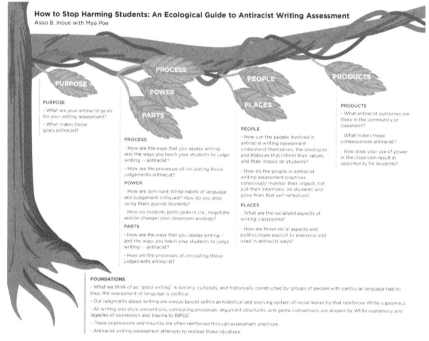

How to Stop Harming Students: An Ecological Guide to Antiracist Writing Assessment
Asao B. Inoue with Mya Poe

View the full-color version online at https://compstudiesjournal.com

Foundations

- What we think of as "good writing" is socially, culturally, and historically constructed by groups of people with particular language habits; thus, the assessment of language is political.
- Our judgments about writing are always bound within an historical and evolving system of racial hierarchy that reinforces White supremacy.
- All writing and style conventions, composing processes, argument structures, and genre conventions are shaped by White supremacy and legacies of oppression and trauma to BIPOC.
- These oppressions and traumas are often reinforced through assessment practices.
- Antiracist writing assessment attempts to redress these injustices.

Purpose

- What are your antiracist goals for your writing assessment?
- What makes those goals antiracist?

Process

- How are the ways that you assess writing—and the ways you teach your students to judge writing—antiracist?
- How are the processes of circulating those judgements antiracist?

Power

- How are dominant White habits of language and judgement critiqued? How do you stop using them against students?
- How do students participate in (i.e., negotiate and/or change) your classroom ecology?

Parts

- How are the ways that you assess writing—and the ways you teach your students to judge writing—antiracist?
- How are the processes of circulating those judgments antiracist?

People

- How can the people involved in antiracist writing assessment understand themselves, the ideologies and histories that inform their values, and their impact on students?
- How do the people in antiracist writing assessment practices consciously monitor their impact, not just their intentions, on students and grow from that self-reflection?

Places

- What are the racialized aspects of writing classrooms?
- How are those racial aspects and politics made explicit to everyone and used in antiracist ways?

Products

- What antiracist outcomes are there in the community or classroom?
- What makes those consequences antiracist?
- How does your use of power in the classroom result in opportunity for students?

Articles

Queering Ethos: Interrogating Archives in the First Year Writing Classroom

Jennifer Ansley

This essay contributes to recent scholarship in queer and feminist rhetorical studies that has argued for a formulation of ethos as a rhetorical practice that centers the rhetor's awareness of their subjective, spatial, material inter-dependence with and accountability to others. My first year writing course, titled "Archiving LGBTQ Lives," became an opportunity to reflect on ar-chival work as a specific context through which we might practice this ap-proach to ethos construction while also considering what it might mean to *queer* ethos. This essay argues that by interrogating the role of the archives in normalizing particular histories and ways of knowing, "Archiving LGBTQ Lives" worked to not only redefine, but to *queer* ethos by asking students to listen to the past in ways that centered their accountability to those who've been historically marginalized along intersecting lines of gender, sexuality, and race, and concludes by offering the scholarly personal narrative as a spe-cific tool for helping students to think critically about their ethical relation-ship to the work of writing and to knowledge production more generally.

In their recent book, *Rethinking Ethos: A Feminist Ecological Approach to Rhetoric*, editors Kathleen Ryan, Nancy Meyers, and Rebecca Jones define a "feminist ecological imaginary" as "a creative and social way of thinking, a living philosophy that better accounts for ethos construction" (3). The con-cept of a feminist ecological imaginary offers a refined definition of ethos that not only considers one's own subject position in relationship to others, but also the "shifting material, cultural and historical situation circulating around rhetorical acts" (5). This definition of ethos reframes our normative understanding of the term, which in the context of classical rhetoric, is often associated with efforts to affirm one's individual credibility and persuasive power, which Ryan, et al. argue lacks a consideration of relationships across difference (5). As an alternative to classical rhetoric, scholarship in the field of feminist rhetorical studies defines ethos as a rhetorical practice interested, instead, in *negotiating* differences across relationships. In her now well-known book, *Rhetorical Listening: Identification, Gender, and Whiteness*, Krista Rat-cliffe offers listening, in particular, as a rhetorical practice that performs "a conscious choice to assume an open stance in relation to any person, text, or culture," proceeding from an "accountability logic" (rather than an attempt to affirm one's one own credibility) and recognizes that "all people necessarily have a stake in each other's quality of life" (17, 26, 31). Together, these important works in feminist rhetorical studies help us approach the work of ethos construction in a way that centers the rhetor's awareness of their subjective, spatial, material interdependence with and accountability to others, and offers listening as a specific practice that might allow us to accomplish that work.

I explored this approach within the context of my first year writing seminar "Archiving LBGTQ Lives." Working with writers in this course became an opportunity to reflect on archival work as a specific context through which we might practice this approach to ethos construction while also considering what it might mean to *queer* ethos. I locate my discussion here in the example of "Archiving LGBTQ Lives," in part, because while Ryan, et al.'s concept of the feminist ecological imaginary emphasizes spatial and material relationships, "queering ethos," as Stacey Waite argues, asks that we also consider our *temporal* location to others (75). Even before encountering Waite's work, questions of temporality struck me as particularly important to consider in work with first year writers, many of whom are still coming to an understanding of the present and future as shaped by the past. In the context of queer studies and queer historiography, in particular, questions of temporality are—given the combination of historical silence and violence surrounding LGBTQ+ experience—also questions of mourning. As Heather Love writes, "The effort to recapture the past is doomed from the start. To reconstruct the past, we build on ruins; to bring it to life, we chase after the fugitive dead" (21). However, Love argues, queer studies scholars have, at the same time, become inadvertently invested in a "linear, triumphalist view of history" that constitutes "a critical compulsion to fix—at least imaginatively—the problems of queer life," making it difficult for us to confront the harms of the past and, by extension, the present (3). For Waite, queer ethos, instead, "calls on us to, as Emily Dickinson might put it, 'dwell in possibility,' to see not only from our own limited positionalities, but to see from elsewhere, to cultivate the ability to imagine elsewhere or otherwise," to imagine alternative futures (72).

In "Archiving LGBTQ Lives," I took a resonant, but slightly different tack than Waite, however. In order to encourage students to "dwell in possibility"—in order to *queer* ethos—and cultivate students' ability to *listen* attentively to the experiences of others across time while maintaining critical attention to where they dwell in historically-constituted relationship to others, I designed "Archiving LGBTQ Lives" with an emphasis on dwelling in the possibilities of *the past* (rather than the future). This essay contributes to the discussion around ethos construction by arguing that by interrogating the role of the archives in normalizing particular histories and ways of knowing, "Archiving LGBTQ Lives" worked to not only redefine, but to *queer* ethos by asking students to listen to *the past* in ways that centered their accountability to those who've been historically marginalized along intersecting lines of gender, sexuality, and race. My goal was for students to—as Eve Sedgwick puts it—imagine not only that the future might be different from the present, but to make it "possible to entertain such profoundly relieving, ethically crucial possibilities as that the past, in turn, could have happened differently than the way it did" (146). This marking of a possible past, Michael de Certeau reminds us, is not only to "make a place for the dead, but to redistribute the space of possibility," and in doing so, "use the narrativity that buries the dead as a way of establishing a place for the living" (100). Understanding Sedgwick and de Certeau's words as a theoretical approach to engaging with archives recognizes both a) that the historical record is fraught with gaps and omissions that potentially undermine claims to credibility and authority that are normatively associated with ethos and b) that we should ask how those omissions might impact our subjective and ethical relationship to our work as writers in the present.

As I make this argument, I begin by offering some context regarding my course design and the working definition of *archives* from which we started. I then reflect on how our discussions of the assigned readings helped us to collaboratively redefine and expand what we mean by *archives*, and I show how questioning the role of archives in the production of knowledge about LGBTQ+ people and communities contributed to students' critical reflection on the ethical stakes of doing archival research. Indeed, throughout this essay, I often make a distinction between "authoritative claims" (that I associate with normative ethos construction) and an ethical approach to working with archival material (that demonstrates an awareness of difference and of how difference has been shaped, in part, through the very work of knowledge production in which all writers are engaged). In response, students most saliently expressed what I call *queer ethos* in the scholarly personal reflections they wrote at the end of the semester. I conclude by offering the scholarly personal narrative as a specific tool for helping students to think critically about their ethical relationship to the work of writing and to knowledge production more generally.

I taught "Archiving LGBTQ Lives" in a WID-based writing program at a private research university where I primarily teach first year writing courses on topics in queer and feminist cultural studies. In these courses, my goal is for students to cultivate, not just writing and research skills, but *habits of mind* that, in addition to those identified by the *Framework for Success in Post-Secondary Writing*, include a sense of the ethical stakes involved in writing for and about marginalized communities; in other words, it is important that my students—many of whom occupy positions of privilege along the lines of race, class, gender, sexuality, and ability—learn to operate from the very account-ability logic that Ratcliffe argues for in *Rhetorical Listening* (1). Owing to a persistent culture of homophobia and a vast loss of life that includes the early years of the AIDS crisis, LGBTQ+ archives are particularly partial, emotional, incoherent, messy, incomplete, and community-based in their origins, making them a unique site for encouraging students to think critically about ethos, particularly given the normative presumption that ethos is constituted via articulations of credibility and authority that, despite the incompleteness of historical records, are often reinforced via archival research. While I did not explicitly frame our project as an opportunity to reflect on "ethos construc-tion," students were consistently asked to pause and reflect on their subjective position in relationship to what they were learning in the archives (knowledge that, again, we know to be incomplete and shaped by histories of discrimi-nation) instead of moving to make authoritative claims based on what they found. In other words, they were asked, again, to *dwell* in the uncertainties and possibilities.

While all archives, including those representing people of color and ethnic minorities, operate as sites of narrative conflict—making available different ways of telling the "truth" of the past—the particular losses and gaps that shape the development of queer archives make them significant as a starting point for understanding one's subjective relationship to the past. As Valerie Rohy writes, queer archives may be "most compelling not as institutions that bestow 'our' names and tell 'our' stories, but as opportunities to observe how the consolations of identity are inextricable from effacement" (358). In other words, queer archives are sites where we are all—regardless of our particular identifications—moved to question fixed notions of community and identity; to ask what materials constitute "legitimate" historical record; and to question how the legitimation of some knowledges has been used to discipline the experiences of others. Queer archives are, then, also ideal sites to confront what Jonathan Alexander and Jacqueline Rhodes refer to as the uncontainable excesses that make "queer" such a challenging subject for composition studies in that, like queerness itself, these archives have "the potential to stretch our sense of not only what *can* be composed, but *how* it can be composed," and to also look at what is *not* composed or *refuses* to be composed (183). These archives move us to question what we think we know about the past and to interrogate the forces that shape both archival records and the stories that we construct out of them; as such, they are also useful for helping students to think critically about knowledge production and the authority of the historical narratives they are composing in their own writing—in short, for queering ethos.

In "Archiving LGBTQ Lives," students worked with: relevant univer-sity archives; several community-based and digital archives, including the community-based Durham LGBTQ+ History Project, Country Queers: A Multimedia Oral History Project, and the Queer Zine Archive Project; and a range of cultural texts that challenge what we mean by archives, including texts like Alison Bechdel's graphic memoir *Fun Home* and Cheryl Dunye's mockumentary, *The Watermelon Woman*. I'll discuss these archives and how students engaged with them in more detail in a moment, but suffice to say that they varied in the conditions of their production, the institutional relationships that help to produce and sustain them, the degrees of community involvement they invite, and the questions they raise about how we know what we think we know about LGBTQ+ lives past and present. This range of materials was also meant to undermine any understanding of archives as fixed, objective, and complete sources of historical knowledge, housed solely in libraries and universities. In the course description included in the syllabus, I wrote: "The goal of this course is not only to explore and contemplate the documents, manuscripts, and ephemera held in these archives, to glean what we can from them about LGBTQ+ life and history, but to also consider how institutional settings, collection practices, and the arrangement of materials—the *composition* of the collections—shape what we think we know about LGBTQ+ people and communities, past and present." In other words, I asked: What are archives? How do they gain their authority? What understanding of minoritized subjects—their histories and knowledges—are produced through different kinds of archives, and as writers and scholars who may or may not belong to these communities, what is our relationship to that body of knowledge and our responsibility to the communities we are writing for, with, and about?

These inquiries were, in turn, an invitation think critically about our work as writers and the stories we tell about marginalized communities, beginning with two assignments that asked students to reflect on the stories they might tell based on what they found in the archives and the relationship between those stories and more mainstream, taken-for-granted narratives of LGBTQ+ life. The first of these two assignment was a 3-4 page document analysis that asked students to choose 3-4 items drawn from collections housed at our university. These collections, which I chose in collaboration with the collection development librarian, Kelly Wooten, included records from Southerners on New Ground; Mandy Carter's Papers; Lady Slipper Records, a Durham, NC-based record label and non-profit organization devoted to promoting women's music; the North Carolina Lesbian and Gay Health Project; and Triangle Community Works. The assignment asked students to "make a focused, arguable claim about what we can learn about LGBTQ+ history, identity, or community based on the documents you've chosen. In other words, what story does this set of documents tell?" The purpose of this assignment, as laid out on the assignment sheet, was to not only practice analyzing primary source material, but to begin developing an awareness that different sets of primary source materials tell different stories that we, as writers, have a hand in composing. The second assignment built on the first by asking students to incorporate secondary source research into their primary source analysis. They were asked to write 5-8 pages that drew their readers' attention to an aspect of LGBTQ+ history that has received less attention. Much of our discussion in the context of this second assignment was on the silences and gaps in the historical record that might have consequences for the arguments we make in our own writing. Listening to these silences and gaps, I argued, can help us question our assumptions about the history of LGBTQ+ life and, in turn, raise questions about our accountability to others. Students wrote, for example, about the lack of historical attention to the experiences of bisexual women, attempts to limit and exclude LGBTQ+ art from public exhibitions in the early years of the AIDS crisis, and the underexamined intersection between early transgender and racial justice movements as exemplified by the work of Street Transvestite Action Revolutionaries (STAR).

I began the reading discussions that paralleled these first two assignments by defining archives as assemblages of primary source materials and objects of analysis, collected in a physical or digital exhibit, in a university library, or in a physical or digital repository accessible to the public at large. My hope was that through our discussions, students would complicate this definition of archives further, and indeed, as we read, they grappled with the more expansive definitions offered by a range of theorists. For instance, in Jack Halberstam's words, archives are not "simply a collection of data" but rather "suggest a discursive field and structure of thinking" (32). In the same vein, Diana Taylor argues in *The Archive and the Repertoire* that the archive functions as "an episteme, a way of knowing, not simply an object of analysis," and we discussed how different writers' understanding of archives shapes different ways of knowing (2003: xvi). We considered formulations of archives offered by scholars that included Anne Cvetkovich, Martin Manalansan, Elspeth Brown, Sara Davidman, and Elsie Chenier, among others. We thought about archives as repositories of information, physical sites, indicators of progress or visibility, registers of fantasy or desire, memorials, articulations of trauma, homes, "safe spaces," documents, performances, artworks, memories, and messes. We also considered collections one would not typically think of as archives, such as the households of undocumented queer immigrants living in New York City or Cheryl Dunye and Zoe Leonard's imagined archive that documents the life of the so-called "Watermelon Woman," the subject of Dunye's 1996 mockumentary. We asked how these ways of knowing resonated with or were different from the ways of knowing we encountered in the university archives.

I began our discussions by emphasizing that although many archives of LGBTQ+ life have been lost due to the historical and systematic marginalization of LGBTQ+ people and the stigma associated with non-normative genders and sexualities, many of the institutional collections that do exist began as community-based projects that insisted on the "involvement of members of the community whose records are in the archives in collecting and accessing their history *on their own terms*" (Wakimoto et al. 295). Over the course of the 20th and 21st centuries, however, many of those collections have become affiliated with colleges and universities or other granting agencies and institutions in order to ensure their survival. This change over time has, in some cases, meant less community involvement in the creation and maintenance of the collections and, often, more limited access for those who do not have academic affiliations. Of course, ensuring the survival of these collections is important and necessary and, as Siobhan Somerville points out, the incorporation of materials documenting LGBTQ+ life into university archives is evidence of the meaningful role that universities played in "the historical production of same-sex sexual cultures" (14). However, as Rod Ferguson reminds us, the management of knowledge about non-normative genders and sexualities also emerged in the late-20th and 21st centuries as a form of "spectacular [affirmation] in the form of rights, benefits, and visibility" that included the development and increased legitimacy of university departments and archives dedicated to minoritarian knowledges (170). Given this tension between universities' roles in the creation of same-sex cultures and the diminishing involvement with and limited access of community members to this institutionalized knowledge, it is worth considering their potentially normalizing and limiting effect on the stories we tell about marginalized communities and people, inadvertent smoothing effect the fissures and gaps that illuminate silences and contradictions in the historical record, and obscuration of less "respectable," more transgressive aspects of LGBTQ+ life.

Marc Stein's essay, "Canonizing Homophile Respectability: Archives, History and Memory," offered us EBSCO's LGBT Life research database as a specific example of the potential normalizing effects that archives can have. Stein argues that the institutionalization of knowledge about LGBTQ+ people in the form of databases and special collections have played a role in privileging the less illicit, less radical aspects of LGBTQ+ life that are part of the community's past and present (66). Stein's principal example of this is historians' tendency to focus on three main periodicals—*ONE Magazine*, *Mattachine Review*, and the *Ladder*—as primary sources for analyzing the homophile movement of the 1950s and '60s. This focus has led to a tendency to "downplay the sexually transgressive elements of homophile activism" that one might uncover in lesser-known, more pornographic texts such as *Drum*, which

Stein reminds us had a significantly larger circulation than the other three texts combined (53). Community-based archives' need for funding helped facilitate the incorporation of many community-based archives into more "legitimate," larger institutional archives and databases, making increased gate-keeping more likely, both in terms of available records and potential access. For example, in order to access the special collections at the New York Public Library, which include some of the most significant historical records related to the early AIDS crisis, one is required to provide an institutional affiliation, project title and description, and references. This fundamentally limits the possibility of community engagement with those records, despite the fact that those records would not exist without community-based archival efforts. We might also consider the potential consequences of, for example, the 2004 renaming of the ONE National Gay & Lesbian Archives and its subsequent absorption into the University of Southern California's library system in 2010 or the opening of the GLBT Historical Society's new museum space in the same year, which was generously funded by corporations organizations that include Levi's, the City and County of San Francisco, and Starbucks.

Of course, community-based collections continue to exist and physical archives continue to act as resources for the LGBTQ+ community in the form of community centers, despite their occasionally fraught relationship to funding structures, granting institutions, and gate-keeping practices. When I worked as a volunteer processing archivist at the ONE Archives in Los Angeles, I witnessed how that space, despite its then newly formalized relationship to the University of Southern California, operated as an event space and site of communal mourning for LGBTQ+ people lost to HIV/AIDS and other forms of violence. We might also consider the expansive collection of ephemera housed in the Lesbian Herstory Archive—archives that Anne Cvetkovich reminds us began on the shelves of Joan Nestle and Deborah Edel's Upper West Side New York City apartment—which now includes lesbian pulp novels, over 600 t-shirts, banners from marches, costumes, sporting equipment, and pornographic materials (240). Today, the Lesbian Herstory Archive is funded, in part, by corporate matching grants and royalties from EBSCO and Thompson Gale Publishing, and in its current location in Park Slope, it continues, in Anne Cvetkovich's words, to "combine private domestic space with public, institutional ones" and "provide an emotional rather than a narrowly intellectual experience" (241). I point to these tensions in the production of, maintenance of, and access to different archives, however, because they are the tensions I wanted students to consider as they composed their own arguments. Rather than moving quickly to making authoritative claims based on what they found in the archives, I wanted them to consider the normalizing structural forces shaping their own knowing and what that might mean for the authority they asserted in their own work.

The linear progressive narrative of gay life and history that Heather Love points to is also potentially reinforced by the arrangement and maintenance of special collections and exhibits. Donald Romesburg has attributed this tendency to the "pressure toward grand progressive narratives," the "consignment of queerness to temporary displays," and the "censorship of non-normative or explicit lives, acts, and representations" (132). As an example, we considered an exhibit documenting the history of LGBTQ+ activism on our campus. While the exhibit importantly centered LGBTQ+ student activism in the history of student life (affirming Somerville's argument regarding the role of universities in the emergence of LGBTQ+ culture and activism in the 20th century), the exhibit nonetheless offered a timeline that tracked the university's expanding gender and sexual inclusivity without regard to the ongoing challenges of LGBTQ+ students, faculty, and staff. Such exhibits risk obscuring the current institutional challenges experienced by LGBTQ+ people and communities by engaging a politics of inclusivity that appropriates difference in service of diversity and inclusion initiatives, rather than meaningfully interrogating gender and sexual norms. When I showed the website associated with the exhibit to students, I framed it as a "composition" grounded, like their own compositions, in a curated selection of materials drawn from the university archives. Our discussion revolved around the questions Romesburg raised for us about whether the exhibit coordinated communities within the university and across the city in order to exhibit the widest array of material; how it articulated community belonging; and where it "made power plain," as Romesburg suggests that "queer" exhibits and archives should (138). During that discussion, one student asked about the audience for the exhibit (such an important question!) and noted that he felt, as a gay student, that the exhibit did not address him, but that it was more interested in promoting the university while failing to recognize the operations of power that shape the experiences of LGBTQ+ student, faculty, and staff at the university, both past and present.

Our rhetorical framing of archives can also influence our encounters with the knowledge found there and students' perceptions of its role in reinforcing their own authority. Despite the messiness and constructedness of all archival knowledge, queer archivist Alana Kumbier points out, for example, that the noun-phrase "*the* archive" as opposed to "archives" operates as a rhetorical gesture that has the potential to fix and stabilize the meaning of *the* archive (Kumbier 12, emphasis added). An understanding of an archive—as monolithic, singular, spatially bounded, and unproblematically reflective of historical truth—implied by this rhetorical gesture also reinforces the expectation that what one gains from the archive is certainty and insight into "others" that affirms the authority of one's writing. Ferguson's essay implicitly offers historical context for this rhetorical positioning of the archives, defining "archives," as they've taken shape in the U.S. academy since the 1960s, as repositories of national culture that, "affirm difference" while nonetheless "keep[ing] it in hand," helping to manage it (166). And indeed, the insight that students might believe they have garnered helps maintain a belief in identities as stable and manageable categories of difference, rather than offering them an opportunity for critical reflection that might destabilize their understanding of concepts like identity and community, and allow them to consider an ethical orientation to their work that raises questions about one's own subjectivity and historical relationship to others. And the work we did to question the definition, boundaries, and make-up of archives themselves led us to also question assertions of scholarly authority offered by others and in turn, ourselves. I designed "Archiving LGBTQ Lives" with the goal of highlighting and creating more opportunities for this kind of reflection, emphasizing the potential for queer archives to make space for emotional memory that might be specific or personal; be fragmented and resist coherent historical narratives; be rife with possibility; and be informed and shaped by, not only documentation of the past, but—to echo the concerns of Waite's work—a desire for another future.

Indeed, the other tension that we grappled with in our discussions was the distinction between LGBTQ+ archives—materials that document the lived experiences of lesbian, gay, bisexual, transgender, and queer-identified people—and what some scholars refer to as queer archives. Queer archives, for me and many queer studies scholars, denote archival repositories and projects whose methods of collection and curation self-consciously attempt to challenge institutional conventions surrounding the collection and organization of archival materials with the intention of encouraging us to think critically about mainstream or taken-for-granted histories and knowledge about LGBTQ+ life. Just as the theoretical term queer moves us to examine, in Eve Sedgwick's terms, "the open mesh of possibilities, gaps, overlaps, dissonances and resonances, lapses and excesses of meaning when the constituent elements of anyone's gender, of anyone's sexuality aren't made (or can't be made) to signify monolithically," so might we refer to those repositories of information that in their very form draw our attention to incoherencies, excesses, and gaps as queer (8). Being attentive to these gaps—or in other words, practicing queer ethos—requires that we be attentive to the incompleteness of our own knowledge and moments in the historical record that might result in uncertainty.

As examples of what we might call queer archives, I introduced students to several digital and community-based projects led by activists, who are not necessarily trained archivists; these included the Queer Zine Archive Project, the Transgender Oral History Project, the Country Queers Multimedia Oral

History Project, the Mobile Homecoming Project, and the Durham LGBTQ+ Oral History Project. As Kumbier notes, these kinds of collections demonstrate that "some queer communities are already actively building archives, self-documenting, inviting community members to help develop collections, teaching others how to archive, and developing culturally-specific practices, principles, and documentation strategies. They are not waiting for archivists to come rescue their collections" (12). I included these community-based projects in the syllabus for "Archiving LGBTQ Lives," not only because they fill gaps in knowledge, but because they highlight archives and the histories that we construct out of them as contested bodies of knowledge. The possibility of narrative conflict, disagreement, and inconsistency are part of the collections themselves.

For example, *Country Queers*, which recently emerged as a podcast, is an "ongoing multimedia oral history project documenting the diverse experiences of rural and small town LGBTQIA+ folks in the U.S.A." that not only troubles dominant urban-centered narratives of LGBTQ+ experience, but also counters assumptions about what life is like for LGBTQ+ people in rural areas (Country Queers). In one interview, Twig Delujé, who identifies as a queer rural trans masculine guy from Hayes, Kansas, living in Pecos, New Mexico, reflects on the different priorities of rural and non-rural queer people:

> I feel like people in cities—I'm going to say, in non-rural areas, for a large part get very, very wrapped up in a lot of politics and a lot of concern around politics not just like governmental, but gender politics… when you're in a rural existence, sometimes you're more concerned about your garden [laughs] or your next meal, or the safety of your pets or your livestock, or just your own safety. (Delujé)

Here, Twig observes an often-unrecognized tension between the material concerns of rural queer people and the political ideals of urban, mainstream queer communities. Twig's narrative and its inclusion in an oral history archive that privileges the voices of rural LGBTQ+ people, operates as a counter-archive that asks us to recognize and sit with this tension, rather than try to resolve it into a coherent narrative of community. By making space for these kinds of tensions, activist archival projects like *Country Queers* offer an opportunity to trouble (or "queer") narratives of identity and community that students might be unconsciously eager to fix into place in their own writing as a way of bolstering their authority as writers. These tensions in the archives are also crucial to engaging students around the question of how we know we know what we know and to encouraging self-consciousness around their own written contributions to the historical and political production of identity knowledges.

We also looked at texts such as Cheryl Dunye's *Watermelon Woman* and discussed cultural archives that exist beyond the library; what the archives cannot tell us; and how different archives might mark the histories they tell as contested. In her mockumentary, *The Watermelon Woman* (1996), Cheryl Dunye investigates the biography of Fae Richards, a black actress from the 1930s, who appears in film credits simply as "The Watermelon Woman." Although Fae Richards is Dunye's fiction (created in collaboration with the artist Zoe Leonard, who produced the fictional photographic archive for Dunye's film), the character symbolizes an actual early 20th century phenomenon in which women of color were disproportionately cast in supporting roles, usually as domestic servants, and then went unnamed in the film credits. As Dunye's invention of *Plantation Memories* (starring Faye Richards) implies, these films were part of what's sometimes referred to as the "*Gone with the Wind* phenomenon," a moment in the 1930s in which 19th century historical melodramas—which include the first adaptation of Louisa May Alcott's *Little Women* (1933); *Camille*, starring Greta Garbo (1936); and *Jezebel*, starring Bette Davis (1938)—exploded in popularity (Donaldson 269). Dunye's mockumentary self-consciously works within this system of historical citation, working backward from her present as a black lesbian filmmaker in 1997, studying a fictional film made in the 1930s that tells a fictional narrative about the 19th century, illustrating for students how cultural texts cumulatively participate in shaping our understanding of the past through both the stories they tell and the stories they do not. *Watermelon Woman* is an example of how cultural texts function as archives and of how an archive might operate as a site of both historical memory and a site of imagined possibility when that archive is incomplete. As Dunye notes in the closing credits, "Sometimes you have to create your own history. *The Watermelon Woman* is fiction."

In the discussion that followed, we spent time reflecting on the gaps and inconsistencies in the archives about which we were writing, particularly in the context of Anne Cvetkovich's writing about the work of filmmaker Jean Carlomusto, who argues that "truth is a hunch" and that to historicize is to tell the truth that is a hunch (255). We discussed using reliable, available evidence to argue for that story, rather than allowing ourselves to be seduced by claims to a singular or coherent truth, particularly when the truth has been obscured by histories of violence against a marginalized community. And indeed, in "Archiving LGBTQ Lives," I was pleased that, over the course of the semester, students were increasingly drawn to and invested in claims like Martin Manalansan's that "mess, clutter, and muddled entanglements are the 'stuff' of queerness, historical memory, aberrant desires, and the archive" and began to listen for the messiness, contradiction, and uncertainty rather than the neatness implied by the boxes of numbered file folders they encountered at the library (94). They looked for the queerness inherent in the archives themselves. As a consequence, students sought out fewer easy answers that affirmed the authority of their own assumptions and were more inclined to interrogate the limits of their own knowledge and the limits of the seemingly coherent, organized, and thorough records they encountered in their research.

Because I was interested in cultivating students' awareness of their ethical relationship to their audiences, encouraging self-questioning in relationship to the knowledge they were helping to produce (and reproduce) was especially important. In "Are the Lips a Grave?" Lynn Huffner, argues for a queer feminist ethics in which ethics is not reducible to authoritative assertions of what does or does not constitute a moral good—the type of assertion we might affirm with normative assertations of ethos—but operates as relational concept in which the "dual burden" is to "first, [acknowledge] harms, and second, [to actively elaborate] alternatives to those harms" (521). Rather than postulating an "ethical agent" whose moral judgments arise from knowing certainty, Huffner's queer feminist ethics is a practice of self-questioning, a historically-contextualized interrogation of one's own subject position and its relationship to the production and erasure of others, that makes space for critical and caring attention to alterity (44). It means, among other things, being honest about and questioning the substance of our own intellectual attachments.

And again, though I didn't frame this for students as a practice of ethos construction per se, it is just that. I also made an effort to model it in the classroom, in large part because I find that too often students' belief in my authority as the instructor translates into a belief in the authority of the archives and the texts we work with (*the* archive that is my syllabus) as evidence of queer experience. Cultivating an awareness of our own affective and political attachments allows us to also be transparent about how they inform the design of our courses and to make our own thought processes available to students for interrogation. In other words, as instructors, we also need to be accountable to others, including our students, by highlighting our subjective relationships to the knowledge being produced in our courses. For example, in "Archiving LGBTQ Lives," I spoke personally and critically about what particular historical materials mean to me as a white, formerly working-class, queer-identified person. The zine collection at the Sallie Bingham Center for Women's History and Culture is, for instance, a collection that I feel personally attached to given my experience of growing up in the '90s, writing poetry for zines, and later creating a queer zine with my best friend as I was negotiating questions about my own sexuality. As part of this anecdote, I acknowledge to my students that the zine as a material artifact of queer youth experience is one that, while personally meaningful to me, is also partly constructed by the expansive archival zine collections that exist most notably at Duke University and Barnard College and the celebratory histories that have been written around them. That history is one that privileges a specifically white queer female youth experience connected to punk culture and the phenomenon of Riot Grrl. But what might it mean—how might it change our understanding of those collections, I ask out loud—to read them in relationship to forms of DIY literature that have sought, for example, to critique systems of power that include policing and prison systems? It might connect those archives, I explain, to a history of social justice movements that more fully include the work and voices of people of color and perhaps decenter white queer youth experience in the history of the genre.

While I understand why some instructors prefer to avoid making personal disclosures or sharing anecdotes in the classroom, I find them crucial to demonstrating the unavoidably affective dimensions of knowledge production. Personal disclosures illustrate how our investments in particular historical materials and narratives can produce pleasure and also lead to critical oversights—to a story that, while not untrue, has ethical implications for our work. Demonstrating for students what it looks like to interrogate our own investments is also central to helping them also come to an understanding of identity and community that is less stable and coherent than historical narratives of LGBTQ+ life often suggest.

The third and final assignment for the course was then an opportunity for my students to make a similar move—not to assert what they knew, but to interrogate their own investments in the material they had worked with during the semester. After becoming familiar with several physical, digital, and community-based archival collections, this final project gave them the option of helping to collect and curate materials for the Durham LGBTQ+ History Project or of curating an archive of their own using a digital content curation tool such as Wordpress or Omeka. This assignment built on the previous two by giving students the opportunity to compose in a different medium, to be a part of the creation and curation of an archive, and to think about how what they had learned from queer theories of the archives might translate to the practice of documenting LGBTQ+ lives. During this assignment, we had visits from Wooten, the collection development librarian for Duke's Sallie Bingham Center for Women's History and Culture, who worked with us all semester; Luke Hirst, the founder and curator of the community-based Durham LGBTQ+ History Project; and Rae Garringer, the founder of the Country Queers Multimedia Oral History Project. Each talked about the challenges and pleasures of collecting and documenting LGBTQ+ experiences in the varying institutional and community contexts in which they work. This was not only a moment for students to learn about the work that archivists do and the different forms it can take, but also a moment for students to further reflect on their own institutional and subjective relationship to the material they were encountering, working with, and helping to organize and make public.

The students then composed a scholarly personal narrative that reflected on precisely those questions—their subjective, intellectual, and ethical relationship to the narratives that emerged from the archives we engaged with, and what they'd gained from their experience of the course. Scholarly personal narrative is self-reflection informed by scholarly research that includes the "unabashed, up-front admission" that your experience has meaning and significance (Nash 24). A meaningful scholarly personal narrative recognizes the degree to which we affect and are affected by others and that social relationships play a role in meaning making (Nash 26). Authors of scholarly personal narrative make their presence known in their writing in a way that is often discouraged by academic discourse more generally, but that I argue is useful for encouraging critical self-reflection among students and essential to the construction of queer ethos. In their essay, "Queer: An Impossible Subject for Composition," Alexander and Rhodes write that "in asking students to create well-articulated, organized, and coherent texts, we ask them to compose themselves—to order their ideas, their presentation, their texts," and, I would add, we encourage them to do this, in part, as a practice of ethos construction—a performance knowing certainty (194). Alexander and Rhodes call, instead, for "a composition that does not always call on us to be composed," that makes room for the "de-compositions of queerness," for the excesses and gaps that produce uncertainty and fewer neat, knowing narratives of self and other (201). The scholarly personal narrative offers the possibility for students to articulate this lack of composure.

By asking my students to end my class with a scholarly personal narrative, then, I asked them to reflect self-consciously and critically on their subjective relationship to the work of knowledge production in relationship to others. The prompt asked: "What significant institutional forces or power dynamics shape the production of LGBTQ+ archives and how do you understand your role as a contributor to these archives?" One student wrote of their personal experience of marginalization within a mainstream LGBTQ+ movement that in recent years had prioritized same-sex marriage as a political goal and how their feelings of marginalization shaped their approach to the course and the archive they built:

> My goal was to create a history more recognizable to me, one that showed queers not marching with corporate sponsors, and labor activists that weren't just straight men. When digging through archives, I sifted through decades of material on the premise that queer lib-

eration is ideologically in line with leftist movements and that the destruction of capitalism is the only way that queer folks, like myself, who are victimized by the cycle of poverty perpetuated in our present economic system, can thrive.

This self-consciousness about the degree to which their archival project was engaged in telling a particular story—one that rested on an arguable premise that they acknowledged their own investment in—also allowed the student to see the limits of the story they told. They recognized, for example, the counter-productivity of understanding socialist and communist circles as necessarily receptive to identity politics, in general, and to consideration of LGBTQ+ issues, in particular. They also acknowledged that their own position as a student at an elite university—with access to both archives and the time to reflect on Marxist theory—as a position of privilege that potentially disconnects them from the material realities and day-to-day lives of, for example, poor transgender people of color. Instead of working to compose a coherent, knowable history that unconsciously reflected their investments, they constructed and then deconstructed their own story as they explored the ethical implications of one narrative versus another.

Other students were even more cognizant of the distance between their realities and the realities of the people and communities whose lives were reflected in the archives, and their scholarly personal narratives became an opportunity to acknowledge that distance and also reconsider their approach to the study of LGBTQ+ identities and communities and their own interpersonal relationships. In a one-on-one meeting with me, one student, unprompted, described her engagement with the archives as a practice in listening. In her essay, she wrote: "In my attempts to advocate for the queer community, I began speaking for them in a misguided attempt to defend those I saw hurting…I forced an injured community to step back and allow me to defend them, because I believed that I could do a better job of it than they could." She arrived at this realization, in part, through her critique of our university's LGBTQ+ history exhibit as a similar, but more institutionally located, example of the degree to which LGBTQ+ people, rather than being heard, have had narratives of progress and liberation imposed up on them. The fact that she understood scholarly work as an opportunity to listen destabilized her own self-understanding, and she used that as an opportunity, in turn, to rethink the ethos of telling others' stories for them. This was a complex and moving outcome of her work, and it is what led me to ultimately reframe my students' encounters with archives as an opportunity for rhetorical listening that has consequences for how students communicate both in their writing and in their day-to-day interactions with others.

Indeed, the scholarly personal narrative has become a tool that I now regularly use in my classes to help students develop a scholarly practice informed by self-awareness, empathy, and the ethical stakes of writing for and about marginalized communities. It is a tool that I have found particularly effective when deployed in the context of course inquiries guided by a desire to question institutional and scholarly authority; to think critically about how writing, research, and documentation can become complicit in the production of what we think we know about marginalized people and their experiences; and to examine gender and sexuality as unstable identity categories that, as Rhodes and Alexander argue, might lead to a queer lack of composure (181). In our critical engagement with how other people's stories had been told and shaped by institutional factors beyond their control, I believe students developed habits of mind in relationship to the archive and the experiential records of others' lives that privileged listening both for what is said and what is not; learned to acknowlede where their assumptions obscure the possibility of hearing and telling another story; and a practiced willingness to acknowledge both what they do not know and what exceeds knowability, rather than to make appeals to authority that fail to constitute ethical scholarly inquiry.

Acknowledgments

Thank you, first and foremost, to my students, who showed up to our work together with impressive commitment and vulnerability. Thanks to Luke Hirst of the Durham LGBTQ+ History Project, Rae Garringer of the *Country Queers* Podcast and Multimedia Oral History Project, and Kelly Wooten of the Sallie Bingham Center for Women's History and Culture at Duke University for their work with my students and for their roles in collecting these important historical records. I'm continually grateful to work in a community of brilliant teachers who encourage and support my pedagogical experiments. In regard to this project, I'm especially appreciative for the feedback of Matt Whitt, Jim Berkey, stef shuster, and Virginia Solomon. And thanks to my reviewers, Stacey Waite and Christine Martorana, whose expertise and generosity helped to refine this piece.

Works Cited

Alexander, Jonathan, and Jacqueline Rhodes. "Queer: An Impossible Subject for Composition." *JAC : a Journal of Composition Theory*, vol. 31, no. 1/2, 2011, pp. 177–206.

Cvetkovich, Anne. *An Archive of Feelings: Trauma, Sexuality, and Lesbian Public Cultures*. Duke UP, 2003.

Certeau, Michele de. *The Practice of Everyday Life*. U of California P, 1984.

Country Queers. "About Country Queers." https://countryqueers.com/about/. Accessed 30 October 2020.

Delujé, Twig. "Twig Delujé. 31. Pecos, NM. July 2014." *Country Queers*, https://countryqueers.com/twig-deluje-31-pecos-nm-7-8-14/. Accessed 30 October 2020.

Donaldson, Susan. "Telling Forgotten Stories of Slavery in the Postmodern South." *Southern Literary Journal,* vol. 40, no. 2, 2008, pp. 267–83.

Executive Summary. *Framework for Success in Postsecondary Writing,* Council of Writing Program Administrators, National Council of Teachers of English, and National Writing Projects, 2011, http://wpacouncil.org/aws/CWPA/asset_manager/get_file/350201?ver=7548

Ferguson, Roderick. "The Queer Ethic and the Spirit of Normativity." *Queer Futures: Reconsidering Ethics, Activism, and the Political,* edited by Elahe Haschemi Yekani, Eveline Kilian, and Beatrice Michaelis, Routledge, 2013, pp. 165–76

Halberstam, Jack. *In a Queer Time and Place: Transgender Bodies, Subcultural Lives.* Duke UP, 2005.

Huffner, Lynn. "Are the Lips a Grave?" *GLQ: A Journal of Lesbian and Gay Studies,* vol. 17, no. 4, 2011, pp. 517–42.

Kumbier, Alana. *Ephemeral Materials: Queering the Archive.* Litwin Books, 2014.

Love, Heather. *Feeling Backward: Loss and the Politics of Queer History.* Harvard UP, 2009.

Manalansan, M. F. "The 'Stuff' of Archives: Mess, Migration, and Queer Lives." *Radical History Review,* vol. 2014, no. 120, 2014, pp 94–107.

Nash, Robert. *Liberating Scholarly Personal Writing: The Power of Personal Narrative.* Teacher's College P, 2004.

Ratcliffe, Krista. *Rhetorical Listening: Identification, Gender, Whiteness.* Southern Illinois UP, 2005.

Rohy, Valerie. "In the Queer Archive: Fun Home." *GLQ: A Journal of Lesbian and Gay Studies,* vol. 16, no. 3, 2010, pp. iv–361.

Romesberg, Don. "Presenting the Queer Past: A Case for the GLBT History Museum." *Radical History Review,* vol. 2014, no. 120, 2014, pp. 131–44.

Ryan, Kathleen, Nancy Myers, Rebecca Jones. *Rethinking Ethos: A Feminist Ecological Approach to Rhetoric.* Southern Illinois UP, 2016.

Sedgwick, Eve. *Tendencies.* Duke UP, 1994.

—. *Touching Feeling: Affect, Pedagogy, Peformativity.* Duke UP, 2003.

Stein, Marc. "Canonizing Homophile Respectability: Archives, History and Memory." *Radical History Review,* vol. 2014, no. 120, 2014, pp. 52-73.

Somerville, Siobahn. "Locating Queer Culture in the Big Ten." *Learning and Teaching: The International Journal of Higher Education in the Social Sciences,* vol. 6, no. 3, 2013, pp. 9-23.

Taylor, Diana. *The Archive and the Repertoire: Performing Cultural Memory in the Americas.* Duke UP, 2003.

Waite, Stacey. "The Unavailable Means of Persuasion: A Queer Ethos for Feminist Writers And Teachers." *Rethinking Ethos: A Feminist Ecological Approach to Rheto-*

ric, edited by Kathleen Ryan, Nancy Myers, and Rebecca Jones. Southern Illinois UP, 2016.

—. *Teaching Queer: Radical Possibilities for Writing and Knowing.* U of Pittsburgh P, 2017.

Wakimoto, Diane, Christine Bruce, and Helen Partridge. "Archivist as Activist: Lessons from Three Queer Community Archives in California." *Archival Science,* vol. 13, no. 4, 2013, pp. 293-316.

The Impact of Critical Community-Engaged Writing on Student Understanding of Audience

Debra Dimond Young and Rachel Morgan

In this study, we examine the use of community-engaged writing pedagogy and the authentic, contextualized writing projects it creates to determine if students better understand the concept of audience and incorporate that foundational knowledge into their writing process. Thematic analysis of student reflections and interviews found students view academic writing as a test of skills, but view community-engaged writing as a product with a purpose in the world. We also learned students need to understand the position of their writing within a rhetorical situation to successfully incorporate the concept of audience into their writing processes. Finally, students revealed they focus most on audience during the revision process and that community-engaged writing provides students with the incentive and rhetorical situation necessary to develop a more impactful revision process. These findings will help composition instructors identify academic results in community-engaged pedagogy, while the process orientation of the study provides a better understanding of how students incorporate the concept of audience into their writing with implications beyond community-engaged writing courses.

Despite instructors' best efforts, students often struggle to understand audience. Having spent their educational lives being taught to write for a teacher, university students often experience difficulty transitioning to contextually based writing. In response, composition scholars have embraced authentic writing assignments as a way to help students better understand writing for a rhetorical situation, and yet, students can still struggle to understand audience. Given this paradox, we wanted to explore why audience rarely exists beyond the teacher or classroom for many students. We were curious if community-engaged writing projects could provide students with experience in the circulation of modern texts through a complex rhetorical ecology impacting the way they think about audience.

In this study, we examine the use of community-engaged writing and the authentic, contextualized writing projects it creates to see if community-engaged writing impacts student understanding of the concept of audience and how they incorporate such foundational knowledge into their writing process. While significant research has been conducted regarding the effectiveness of community-engaged learning on student civic and personal development, the scholarship regarding the impact of community-engaged learning on the development of course content knowledge is growing. To build on that scholarship, we examined the writing processes of students in community-engaged and non-community-engaged sections of the same first year writing course. We used thematic analysis of student reflections and interviews to provide a holistic view of the impact of community-engaged writing on student understanding and application of audience.

The results were striking. Reflections and interviews indicate students view academic writing as a test of skills, but view community-engaged writing as a product with a purpose in the world. We also found traditional assignments did not help students understand the position of their writing within a rhetorical situation, whereas community-engaged writing did. Finally, we found students focus most on audience during the revision process and that authentic writing assignments, like community-engaged writing, provide students with the incentive and rhetorical situation necessary to develop a more authentic revision process. These findings help composition instructors identify academic results in community-engaged pedagogy, while the study's process orientation provides a better understanding of how students incorporate the concept of audience with implications beyond community-engaged courses.

Critical Community-Engaged Writing

Recent research shows that community-engaged learning, like other forms of problem-based learning, can be academically rigorous and beneficial to student learning in addition to helping students understand their community and develop a sense of social responsibility (Eppler et al.; McNenny; Rosinski and Peeples), positively impacting general academic performance, values, self-efficacy, leadership, choice of a service career, and plans to participate in service after college (Astin et al.; Eyler et al.; Myers–Lipton; Osborne).

When examining community engagement specifically in composition courses, it helps to look at Thomas Deans's foundational work. Deans divides community-engaged writing into three categories: writing about the community, writing for the community, and writing with the community. Our study utilized a "writing for" format, which works in conjunction with a community partner to create materials that help the partner fulfill its mission (Deans, *Writing Partnerships*). While scholarship examining the effect of community engagement on how students learn to write is emerging, existing studies have found notable improvements in student persuasive writing over traditional composition courses (Wurr), a positive and statistically significant difference between research papers written in community-engaged writing classrooms and those written in traditional classrooms (Feldman et al.), and a recognition of writing as a public and social act (Cushman; Iverson). Building on this body of knowledge is important because understanding if and how community-engaged pedagogy impacts course-specific learning is essential to justify the continuation and/or expansion of the practice. Composition instructors, as a whole, tend to value holistic education that promotes critical thinking, leadership, and self-efficacy (all demonstrated benefits of community engagement), but in the end, we teach writing. If community engagement can provide holistic benefits *and* provide a better way to teach writing, then the field is stronger for knowing.

Audience

Audience is considered a threshold concept for first year writers, and yet, despite its foundational nature, students often struggle to understand the impact of audience on writing. Perhaps the issue lies with the ever-evolving view of audience by scholars and, thus, the ever-evolving presentation of audience in the classroom. A look back at the scholarship demonstrates how this fairly innocuous term belies a deeply complex concept. Audience is a fiction (Ong) or a shifting set of roles for writer and reader (Reiff). Audience can be addressed or invoked (Ede and Lunsford), a set of contexts (Park, "The Meanings of 'Audience'"), or the constantly changing ecology in which students write (Cooper 368). It's vital for students to understand the rhetorical elements of purpose, audience, and context, but seeing those elements as separate is simply not plausible in our globally connected world (Chaput; Edbauer) and attempting to separate them masks fluidity of texts (Edbauer 20). The question isn't really one of audience, but of circulation. It's not enough to analyze or understand delivery to an audience; production must be understood because that is where a "hierarchy of knowledge" is created (Trimbur 210). As a text circulates through production and delivery, it is not in search of an audience, but rather produces a series of identities and relationships which can be seen in retrospect as audiences (Biesecker). It is only through interaction with a text that a public emerges; it is impossible to create a text for a specific audience, because the audience doesn't exist in the abstract (Warner).

No wonder students struggle.

The academic environment in which students write only adds to the challenge, since the very nature of academic writing separates authors from environment (Reid and Kroll 17). Academic writing can be seen less as a form of writing and more as a form of testing, requiring students to demonstrate mastery of course objectives. Students, masters of the writing-as-test format, understand that the audience is always the instructor, no matter what the assignment may say, and they write accordingly (Britton; Reid and Kroll). The classroom removes the concept of audience from the writing process because assignment design makes audience extraneous (Park, "Analyzing Audiences"

479). This has led to a push for courses to feature a variety of authentic, contextualized writing assignments to help students break out of the writing-as-test mentality (Bacon; Reid and Kroll). Community-engaged writing, particularly projects that follow Deans's "writing for" model, can provide precisely the type of contextually-based, authentic writing assignments.

Study Design

Participants for this study were drawn from four sections of a first year, integrated communication course at a mid-sized, midwestern university. Cornerstone is a one-year, first year cohort class combining content of the oral communication and composition courses required by the university. There were twenty-six sections of Cornerstone in the 2018-19 academic year, and the four sections we taught became our pool of potential participants. We each taught one section using critical community-engaged writing pedagogy and one section without the community component. We partnered with two community-service organizations to collaboratively create a narrative writing assignment that met course goals and served an important need for our organizational partners, keeping with the core tenets of critical service-learning to equalize the needs of the community organization and the needs of students. Other than the involvement of a community partner, each instructor designed her two sections to be identical in structure and assignments. While there were differences between the sections presented by the two instructors, we worked collaboratively to minimize differences. To ensure we met ethical standards, all interaction between instructor and student, including consent and interviews, were conducted by the opposite instructor, and we did not know which students in our classes were participating until after grades for the studied assignment were submitted.

There were forty-one students in the two non-community-engaged, or control, sections, and of those, twenty-one students consented to participate. There were forty-two students in the community-engaged sections, and eighteen consented to participate. Four students left the university mid-study, leaving nineteen control and sixteen community-engaged participants. Students did not receive extra credit or other benefits from participating in the study. At the time of the study, community-engaged courses were not specially identified by the university during registration, so the students did not know they would be participating in a community-engaged course until the first day of class, alleviating a common concern with community-engaged studies—that students who select community-engaged courses are somehow different from students who choose more traditional course structures.

Because Cornerstone is an integrated communication class, it features a rhetoric-heavy curriculum not always found in composition classes. Throughout the course, we teach foundational concepts of classical rhetoric including the rhetorical triangle, elements of persuasion, and logical fallacies. We present writing as a "social and rhetorical activity" with interconnecting elements of audience, purpose, and context (Roozen 17). In addition to teaching the fundamentals of rhetoric, the course also focuses on different genres. Leading up to the narrative assignment studied, all sections discussed the parts of a story, read model examples of narrative, and analyzed the ways those models did or did not conform to the genre. The genre content tied back to the discussion of rhetorical situation, as part of the analysis focused on the differing purpose, audience, and context for the narratives being discussed. All sections of Cornerstone studied featured the same core curriculum, so all students, community-engaged and control, received the same course content. While all sections read model autobiographical narratives, the control sections also read oral histories, and the community-engaged sections read model narratives from their community partner and other local nonprofit agencies.

Students in the control sections were asked to interview a person of their choice, learn stories from their lives, and write a narrative incorporating one or more of those stories. This assignment mirrors a standard narrative assignment given in countless composition classes. To help students think about the rhetorical situation for their writing, they were led through exercises to define an audience and purpose for the narrative prior to writing.

The students in the community-engaged sections participated in a common "writing for the community" assignment. Each section was paired with a different community partner. One partner provided housing assistance in the community, and the other provided a variety of services to low-income and homeless members of the community. The two partner organizations requested help writing narratives of their volunteers, clients, and staff to use for publicity purposes in newsletters, fundraising materials, and/or websites. Students had already been exposed to the larger issues facing their interview subjects in a previous research assignment focused on the problems of homelessness, income inequality, and food instability to establish context for the community partner.[1] At the beginning of the narrative assignment, a member of the partner organization spoke to the two community-engaged classes to provide organizational background and information. The partners told students some narratives could be chosen for use in organizational publicity materials and provided the instructors with a list of interview subjects and their availability, from which students selected their subject and arranged an interview. Just as with the control class, the students in the community-engaged sections interviewed their subject, attempting to elicit stories of their life, volunteer, or work experiences, and wrote the narratives. The students in the community-engaged sections also worked through the same rhetorical situation exercises as the control classes to establish the audience, purpose, and context for their writing.

When the narrative assignment was submitted, the students in all four sections completed a written reflection. Students in both groups were asked to reflect on their understanding of audience and how they applied this understanding to their writing process. Across all four sections, students were required to complete all aspects of the assignment, including the reflection, regardless of participation in the study.

Once the assignment concluded and grades were recorded, we coded the reflections using theme analysis to develop interview questions (Braun and Clarke; Tracy; van Manen). We observed repetition after very few interviews but continued to interview students until theoretical saturation was realized (Tracy). In total, we interviewed seven students from the control group and seven students from the community-engaged group. At the conclusion of the interview process, we coded the transcripts through a detailed thematic analysis process, looking for commonalities in responses that could be developed into themes.

Results and Implications

Speaking with students and reading their reflections, it rapidly became clear that all students understood the textbook definition of *audience*. Students were able to articulate the concept well, some almost quoting the textbook. As we reviewed the transcripts, reflections, code book, and analytical memos, differences between community-engaged and control students became clear, and three themes emerged from the data: the difference between what Joy Reid and Barbara Kroll call "writing-as-test" and what we call "writing-as-product," the need to see the rhetorical situation as a whole, and the timing of audience consideration within the students' writing processes. In this section, we will explore these three themes in depth, concluding with the implications emerging from this data.

Theme 1: "Writing-as-test" vs. "Writing-as-product"

A myriad of writing scholars have argued that academic writing should be contextualized. Reid and Kroll argue that students writing without context struggle to see writing as a rhetorical situation, since, "(Students) realized that despite whatever 'audience' may be assigned . . . the specter of the teacher–evaluator remains the 'real' and most important audience, and the purpose of their writing is to demonstrate their ability to produce what the teacher expects for a certain grade" (Reid and Kroll 19). Lisa Mastrangelo and Victoria Tischio found similar results as interviews indicated their students "had become habituated to seeing writing as an empty, rule–driven activity, especially in educational settings" (Mastrangelo and Tischio 39). Our research supports both findings and offers a potential solution in the form of community-engaged writing.

Students in the control sections clearly saw the narrative assignment as a test of skills and talked about how their instructor and classmates would read their narratives for grading or peer review, but would go on, in the same breath, to say their narratives had no audience. Even if they said the instructor was the audience, they didn't see her as a "real" audience. Ethan wrote about this issue in his reflection:

> I had to understand that my main audience was just gonna [sic] be my professor, so it kinda [sic] went against what we learned in class a little bit because your audience is usually a certain group of people and not just one specific person, and you aren't just trying to meet the requirements. . . . In general, we didn't have to worry about our audience a whole lot because the only people that were going to read the paper would be the professor and maybe one or two other people.

Overall, students argued instructors aren't "real" audiences because they read primarily to grade. Without knowing it, these students echoed Reid and Kroll's concept of writing-as-test. As Jasper said in his interview, "If I was writing for a campus newspaper, I guess I'd have to cover quite a variety of students and even teachers, professors. If I'm just writing for the class, then I really just have to do it for the grade and for the professor." The students understood the concept of audience and knew audience impacts writing choices, but they simply didn't apply audience to the writing for class.

From the control group, there were two notable exceptions to this finding; Eliza and Cora spoke eloquently about the intended audience for their writing. Both of these students chose to interview people important to them and whose stories they had strong motivation to document. Eliza wrote about her grandmother, a woman she clearly idolized. Cora wrote about a traumatic incident that happened to a dear friend. Both women spoke about how writing for their specific audiences impacted word choices, organizational structure, and motivation, clearly articulating a difference between the writing they did for this project and the writing they typically did for class. For example, Cora stated the assignment was different because she wanted to document an important moment for her friend when, "in the past I've only written just to get a grade or for myself." From their responses, it seemed both Cora and Eliza applied the concept of audience to their writing because they found a way to separate this writing from the standard writing-as-test assignment.

The community-engaged students echoed the control students when we asked about their "typical" classroom writing experiences. Both groups spoke and wrote about how classroom writing usually fits the writing-as-test model. Charlotte articulated the thoughts of many, "Whenever I've written, it was always just for the teacher, and so I was just, like, what can I do to get the best grade?" While community engagement didn't change the students' view of academic writing as a form of testing, it did provide them with a new paradigm to see writing as a product that can be used for a purpose beyond getting a grade.

Time and again, the community-engaged students differentiated classroom writing from their community-engaged writing experience. The first distinction most students noted was the clarity of audience. Thea felt writing for such a well-defined audience helped by, "…taking that big abstract idea of audience and narrowing it down to 'this is who we want to address and how we want to do that,'" bringing the concept of audience out of the textbook and into her writing. Understanding the characteristics of a specific group of people to target with their writing resonated with students, but not as much as understanding how the piece could impact the partner organization. Most students visited their partner site, and all spoke extensively with someone directly impacted by the organization, so they knew the value of the organization. Laura said, while she is a dedicated student, the project gave her incentive to try even harder: "Someone else is going to read this, and it's going to impact their thoughts of the organization, so I wanted to give them a good paper."

The contextual nature of the writing seems to take the assignment out of writing-as-test and into what we call writing-as-product. To be clear, we are using the term "product" to indicate an item that has a use beyond the classroom, not an assignment focused solely on the end result at the expense of process. As many community-engaged writing scholars have found, our students began to see writing as a social action that exists and has the potential to impact the world (Cushman; Heilker; Mathieu and George). This change helped students shift their view of writing away from a test good only for a grade and toward a product with an actual purpose in the world.

Theme 2: The Rhetorical Situation Should Be Considered as a Whole

Our students thought of academic writing as a test rather than a product due to what they saw as the lack of authentic audience but also because of the lack of a purpose or context. While a classroom assignment is a rhetorical situation of sorts, students didn't perceive it as one, causing the writing assignment to reinforce the "writing-as-test" model. Students simply saw academic writing as "spitting out what I learned in class," making it extraordinarily difficult for students to apply the concept of audience to their writing.

The community-engaged writing students, however, saw writing for their partner organization as writing for an "actual" audience, purpose, and context, so they were better able to articulate how they incorporated audience. They could not, however, separate audience from purpose and context very well. Community-engaged writing students wrote and spoke frequently about how their work was for "more than a grade" or how their writing would help their partner organization and community, demonstrating a focus on purpose. Students also spoke of specific choices they made to ensure they were being respectful to their subject or to focus on one important aspect of a subject's story that made their writing more appealing to their audience and ultimately help their partner organization achieve its purpose. For example, Rose defined her audience as potential volunteers and the purpose of her communication as recruitment. She unknowingly echoed Park in her interview when she explained how the audience informed her purpose and vice versa. Rose attempted to center her subject and her subject's experiences with the partner organization as a way to show the benefits of volunteering for the organization, choosing to focus on her subject's Christian faith because she thought "that can connect a lot of Christian-oriented people who want to (volunteer) as well." The contextual writing situation helped the community-engaged students consider all elements of the rhetorical situation when shaping their writing.

We believe an important finding for non-community-engaged instructors can be found in the exceptions within the control group. As we stated previously, two control students, Cora and Eliza, reported having a defined audience for their writing and using that audience to drive their writing choices. Cora defined her audience as her friend and wrote with the purpose of documenting a traumatic event so her friend could have a record of events over which she had triumphed. With this clear and very well-defined audience and purpose in mind, Cora approached her writing differently than she would in a typical academic setting because, "This is not my story; it's someone else's story, too." As she wrote, Cora found that her extremely close relationship with her subject actually made writing challenging, because she kept reverting to writing the story from her own perspective as a witness: "I was more of like a second hand. Like, I was witnessing and helping her go through it, so I had my own things I wanted to add in, but I was, like, it's not my story. It's her story." Throughout the revision process, Cora reported returning to the story to ensure it remained from her friend's viewpoint. She also reported selecting details and words carefully to ensure her friend could remember all she wanted to recall without being triggered by unnecessary but harmful information.

Our community-engaged students could successfully incorporate the concept of audience in part because their communication existed within a defined rhetorical situation, but Cora and Eliza worked to establish a complete rhetorical situation for themselves. This clarity of audience, purpose, and context helped the community-engaged students, Eliza, and Cora all become "engaged in purposeful communication" by making specific choices during their writing process (Park, "Analyzing Audiences" 483–84).

Theme 3: Students Think About Audience When They Revise

Reading the reflections, we were struck by how many students, both community-engaged and control, claimed to consider audience throughout the writing process. We thought it was important to explore this early finding in the interviews, so we asked students to think about audience and what choices were impacted by that consideration. We found that while many students claimed to think about audience throughout the process, only a few of the community-engaged writing students could actually articulate specific examples from early in their writing process. Those students spoke of using their rhetorical situation to shape interview questions rather than using it in the early stages of writing, making audience consideration more of a pre–writing activity than a drafting activity. The vast majority of community-engaged and control students described using their audience to make specific writing decisions during the revision process, supporting findings that most writers, novice and experienced, don't consider audience until revision (Rafoth). While this finding is useful, a closer examination of interview responses provides more nuance to the data.

Students in the control group described using audience as a way to appeal to the instructor and earn a higher grade. Most control students spoke of creating a first draft by dumping all the information they had from their interviews into some written form and then returning for a single pass of revision where they considered word choice and generally tried to make their narratives appealing. Liam summed up the thoughts of many students when he said consideration for his instructor led him to, "…try to use a larger vocabulary, not much humor, and use the rubric as my outline to maximize points earned." In other words, the students did not describe considering an audience, so much as a rubric, following the rules of writing-as-test. Still, consideration for the rubric did lead most control students to make specific decisions during a brief revision or editing process.

An examination of the community-engaged writing group plus Cora and Eliza, highlighted a different approach to incorporating audience. Since these students had a complete rhetorical situation to consider, a few utilized that information during their pre-writing process and shaped their interview questions based on the narrative they knew they needed to write. Those students spoke of asking their subjects for particular types of stories or for descriptions of emotions because they knew that type of information would help them appeal to their audience and achieve their purpose. Like the control students, the community-engaged writing students did an initial dump of information for the first draft, but unlike the control students, the community-engaged students described an extensive revision process where they made multiple passes, specifically thinking about their audience and purpose as they changed perspective, organized stories, and selected language they felt would appeal to their audience. Rose described her initial draft as "word vomit" because she "wasn't thinking in that right mindset" of her rhetorical situation. As she began to revise, Rose described a continuous conversation with herself:

> I had to kind of step back and reword some things that I originally wrote and stuff like that. I needed to say, "Go back to (partner organization). Go back to (partner organization)." ... Just go back to, "This is for (partner organization), this is because of (partner organization)." Instead of being, "This is really great. The end," I'd have to delete a sentence and be like, "Okay, what was I trying to say?" and rephrase it so that it made sense with my purpose and with who I was writing to, rather than what I wanted to write about or what I felt more ... I think the revising part was very crucial to help me to stay on task and keep [the writing] for its purpose.

Multiple community-engaged writing students described a similar internal conversation as a way to revise their writing with focus on audience and purpose. Many described an increased motivation to rework their writing so it could be of use to their partner organization and that motivation helped them focus through multiple revisions. For the community-engaged students in this study, seeing their writing as a part of a larger rhetorical context, as something that could help their partners do good in the world, provided them with motivation to revise.

Implications

The three themes found in this research provide a number of important implications for composition instructors. Not surprisingly, these findings reinforce the call for authentic, contextual writing situations. The writing-as-test mentality is extraordinarily hard to break because it is so ingrained in students from their earliest education. Even the community-engaged writing students, who were working within an actual rhetorical situation, reported a difficult time breaking free from thinking of writing as a test of skills.

We must acknowledge that one reason the writing-as-test mentality is difficult for students to shake is because it is always, at least partially, true. Even contextualized writing is used for assessment purposes, and students know that. In our classes, we followed Deans's recommendation and worked with our partners to ensure our assessment criteria was based on their needs, so students in the community-engaged sections knew meeting the needs of their partner was key to their success, but that still frames writing as a test of skills.

Our first theme suggests that while community-engaged writing doesn't eradicate the student narrative that writing is only for a teacher, it does seem to disrupt that narrative by helping students incorporate a writing-as-product mindset in a way most control students couldn't. To use Deans's activity theory terminology, our community-engaged writing students were able to place their work in multiple activity systems simultaneously, while the control students remained in the academic system alone (Deans, "Shifting Locations, Genres, and Motives: An Activity Theory Analysis of Service-Learning Writing Pedagogies"). This finding echoes recent work indicating community-engaged writing helps students develop a flexibility of mind that increases their willingness to adapt to different writing situations (Pinkert and Leon). If we want students to see writing as a life skill and not a form of testing, we need to create authentic, contextually-based writing opportunities that allow students to develop writing skills in multiple activity systems. Community-engaged writing assignments that follow the "writing for" model clearly provide that opportunity, but Cora and Eliza demonstrate even traditional assignments can be shaped to provide context. The fact that all control students completed exercises designed to identify an authentic rhetorical situation for their writing and only two of the participants managed to do so indicates the difficulty of breaking the writing-as-test mentality.

Perhaps the difference is that Cora and Eliza found an audience, purpose, and context for their writing, which other control students reported struggling to do. Thus, our second theme shows that students need to understand their place within a complete rhetorical ecology, not just define a specific audience. The community-engaged writing students, Cora, and Eliza spoke of audience, purpose, and context as intertwined elements that impacted their writing process. Community-engaged writing students who initially identified an audience but not a purpose reported struggling until they figured out how and where their writing could be used. A few control students initially reported wanting to write for a specific audience, but they couldn't identify a purpose or context and soon shifted back into writing for the instructor and rubric. There is a great opportunity for future research to understand why some students are able to make this shift with traditional assignments while others struggle.

And finally, our last theme, understanding how and when students incorporate the rhetorical situation into their writing process could have great impact on composition pedagogy. While all the students reported revising their work, what the control students described was really the half-hearted revision and editing frequently found in composition classrooms: looking over the work one or two times, changing a few words, and fixing the commas. The community-engaged writing students reported splitting the final stages of their writing process into a true revision process followed by editing. They reported changing the perspective of their writing to reflect their subject's viewpoint, reorganizing sections of the writing in order to best appeal to their readers, and making specific vocabulary and tone choices to reflect the needs of their partners, often over multiple drafts. Composition instructors frequently note the lack of revision in student writing, especially with first year students, so this finding is substantial.

The community-engaged writing students cited the need to help their partner organization rather than "just writing for a grade" as the motivation behind their revision, but the fact that Cora and Eliza also developed a revision process indicates this finding isn't limited to community-engaged writing assignments and the motivation might not be exclusively tied to the rhetorical situation. We considered whether our partnership with a community organization impacted the way we shaped the revision process for our students, thus resulting in a different revision outcome. Our approach to revision is very dynamic. As writing instructors, both of us teach revision as conversation, much like the situated workplace writing described by Aviva Freedman and Christine Adam as "attenuated authentic participation" (45). All students received feedback from peers, peer mentors,[2] and instructors as they worked through their drafting process. The only difference in the revision process for the community-engaged and the control students occurred in Deb's community-engaged section when her partner came to class to answer questions and provide feedback, giving those students one more voice in their revision process. Since all students were guided through the same dynamic, conversational approach to revision, the process seems unlikely to have impacted the outcome.

Deans argues that community-engaged writing students often become deeply attached to their partner organization and the staff they work with, and that connection provides a great deal of motivation for their work (Deans, *Writing Partnerships*). That connection to subject could certainly explain why Cora and Eliza acted more like the community-engaged writing students than the control students, as both women expressed a deep connection with their interview subjects. Still, there are reasons to think that connection is not the main source of motivation our revision findings. First, all students, control and community-engaged, expressed a desire to be respectful of their interview subject and to be true to their story. Since the control students were able to select their subjects, most chose to speak to people who were important to them. Many students spoke of using the assignment as a way to learn more about family history that was not openly discussed. These students had deep connections to their subjects and yet they still functioned in a writing-as-test mentality with minimal revision based on the rubric.

The community-engaged students, on the other hand, only met with their interview subjects one or twice in order to conduct the interview and therefore did not develop an ongoing relationship. While the students met with an organizational representative, contact was fairly limited. In fact, Deb's representative announced she was making a career change and leaving the organization after meeting with students to provide feedback, so the students knew she wouldn't be the person reading their final work. While students likely found inspiration in their partner organization and interview subject, they didn't work with either enough to develop the types of deep relationships Deans and others describe in direct-service community projects. Such inspiration may have provided additional motivation for students to revise; however, it wasn't a reason they articulated in our interviews.

Instead, our community-engaged students frequently spoke of the pride they felt in helping their partner organization address community issues. This is part of what we have described as seeing their writing as more than a test of skills, but as a product that has the ability to make change. It was, in part, this frequent expression of pride that drew our conclusions back to the impact rhetorical situation and audience have on the revision process. Many of our control students felt a deep connection to their interview subjects, but other than Cora and Eliza, they struggled to find a purpose, context, or audience for their writing outside the classroom. As such, their revision process was attuned to the audience they felt most important: the rubric. Our community-engaged writing students may have felt a connection to their subjects, but they definitely felt pride in the fact that their writing was going to impact the world beyond the classroom. They saw how their writing helped to reach an audience, achieve a purpose, and fit within a context, and that helped them find the motivation to engage in a dynamic revision process. Connection may have been a factor in that motivation, but without a clear understanding of rhetorical situation and audience, it wasn't enough to move students to revise.

The fact that community-engaged writing students reported considering their audience in their writing process during prewriting and revision is also important for composition instructors to understand because these students used their rhetorical situation to shape their interview process, indicating the initial focus on the rhetorical situation paid off. However, finding that all the students dropped their knowledge of their rhetorical situation during their initial draft and picked it back up in revision indicates the need to draw students back to the rhetorical situation as they write. This finding is not surprising; it fits both the research (Rafoth) and the more colloquial call for writers to embrace the "shitty first draft" (Lamott). It does, however, call instructors to make the rhetorical situation explicit during the revision process, as it appears to both shape and motivate revision.

Conclusion

There is a great deal more to learn about the impact of community-engaged pedagogy on student writing. This was a small study at a single university, so to truly understand the impact of community-engaged pedagogy, additional data should be collected and examined. It would also be useful to learn if the results of this study are specifically attributable to community-engaged writing or if other authentic, contextual writing pedagogies would lead to similar results.

Even with these limitations, the findings are significant, suggesting that community-engaged writing pedagogy helps students better understand and apply the threshold rhetorical principal of audience. Community-engaged "writing for" assignments help students break out of a writing-as-test mentality by providing them with the authentic rhetorical situation they need to apply the concept of audience to their writing in a way that helps them develop writing that has more audience relevance and clarity of purpose. Working with a community partner to create a writing product that helps the partner achieve their goals provided enough motivation to push students to develop a true revision process, changing tone, perspective, and structure of their writing. Finally, understanding that students use the concept of audience most during their revision process has implications for all composition instructors. Critical community-engaged writing pedagogy has demonstrated a powerful ability to develop community-engaged students, and our findings indicate community-engaged writing pedagogy also helps students understand core rhetorical writing concepts and develop stronger revision practices as well.

Notes

1. The control students also did a research-based informative speech, but their topics were related to other readings we were using in class.

2. A unique aspect of the Cornerstone course is that an upper-class student participates in the course as a Peer Mentor, providing social, emotional, and academic support to the students in the class.

Works Cited

Astin, Alexander W., et al. "How Service Learning affects Students." *Higher Education*, 2000, http://digitalcommons.uomaha.edu/slcehighed/144.

Bacon, Nora. "Building a Swan's Nest for Instruction in Rhetoric." *College Composition and Communication*, vol. 51, no. 4, 2000, pp. 589–609.

Biesecker, Barbara A. "Rethinking the Rhetorical Situation from within the Thematic of 'Différance.'" *Philosophy & Rhetoric*, vol. 22, no. 2, 1989, pp. 110–30.

Braun, Virginia, and Victoria Clarke. "Using Thematic Analysis in Psychology." *Qualitative Research in Psychology*, vol. 3, no. 2, 2006, pp. 77–101.

Britton, W. Earl. "What Is Technical Writing?" *College Composition and Communication*, vol. 16, no. 4, 1965, pp. 113–16.

Chaput, Catherine. "Neoliberalism and the Overdetermination of Affective Energy: Neoliberalism and the Overdetermination of Affective Energy." *Philosophy & Rhetoric*, vol. 43, no. 1, 2010, pp. 1–25.

Cooper, Marilyn M. "The Ecology of Writing." *College English*, vol. 48, no. 4, 1986, pp. 364–375.

Cushman, Ellen. "The Rhetorician as an Agent of Social Change." *College Composition and Communication*, vol. 47, no. 1, 1996, pp. 7–28.

Deans, Thomas. "Shifting Locations, Genres, and Motives: An Activity Theory Analysis of Service–Learning Writing Pedagogies." *The Locations of Composition*, edited by Christopher J. Keller and Christian R. Weisser, State U of New York P, 2007, pp. 289–306.

—. *Writing Partnerships: Service–Learning in Composition*. National Council of Teachers of English, 2000.

Edbauer, Jenny. "Unframing Models of Public Distribution: From Rhetorical Situation to Rhetorical Ecologies." *Rhetoric Society Quarterly*, vol. 35, no. 4, 2005, pp. 5–24.

Ede, Lisa, and Andrea Lunsford. "Audience Addressed/Audience Invoked: The Role of Audience in Composition Theory and Pedagogy." *College Composition and Communication*, vol. 35, no. 2, 1984, pp. 155–71.

Eppler, Marion A., et al. "Benefits of Service–Learning for Freshmen College Students and Elementary School Children." *Journal of the Scholarship of Teaching and Learning*, vol. 11, no. 4, Dec. 2011, pp. 102–15, https://files.eric.ed.gov/fulltext/EJ956756.pdf.

Eyler, Janet, et al. "The Impact of Service–Learning on College Students." *Michigan Journal of Community Service Learning*, vol. 4, no. 1, 1997, pp. 5–15, http://hdl.handle.net/2027/spo.3239521.0004.101.

Feldman, Ann M., et al. "The Impact of Partnership–Centered, Community–Based Learning on First Year Students' Academic Research Papers." *Michigan Journal of Community Service Learning*, vol. 13, no. 1, 2006, pp. 16–29, https://files.eric.ed.gov/fulltext/EJ843844.pdf.

Freedman, Aviva, and Christine Adam. "Write Where You Are: Situating Learning to Write in University and Workplace Settings." *Transitions: Writing in Academic and Workplace Settings*, edited by Patrick Dias and Anthony Paré, Hampton P, 2000, pp. 31–60.

Heilker, Paul. "Rhetoric Made Real: Civic Discourse and Writing beyond the Curriculum." *Writing the Community: Concepts and Models for Service–Learning in Composition*, edited by Linda Adler–Kassner et al., Stylus, 2006.

Iverson, Chris. "The Long–Term Effects of Service–Learning on Composition Students." *Reflections: A Journal of Community–Engaged Writing and Rhetoric*, vol. 19, no. 2, Spring 2020, pp. 11–37. https://reflectionsjournal.net/wp–content/uploads/2020/03/V19.N2.Iverson.pdf.

Lamott, Anne. *Bird by Bird*. Anchor Books, 1995.

Mastrangelo, Lisa S., and Victoria Tischio. "Integrating Writing, Academic Discourses, and Service Learning: Project Renaissance and School/College Literacy Collaborations." *Composition Studies*, vol. 33, no. 1, 2005, pp. 31–53.

Mathieu, Paula, and Diana George. "Not Going It Alone: Public Writing, Independent Media, and the Circulation of Homeless Advocacy." *College Composition and Communication*, vol. 61, no. 1, 2009, pp. 130–49.

McNenny, Gerri. "Helping Undeclared Majors Chart a Course: Integrating Learning Community Models and Service Learning." *Reflections: A Journal of Writing, Service–Learning, and Community Literacy*, vol. 2, no. 2, 2002, pp. 56–70, https://reflectionsjournal.net/wp–content/uploads/2020/05/V2N2.McNenny.Gerri_.pdf.

Myers–Lipton, Scott J. "Effect of a Comprehensive Service–Learning Program on College Students' Level of Modern Racism." *Michigan Journal of Community Service Learning*, vol. 3, no. 1, 1996, pp. 44–54, http://hdl.handle.net/2027/spo.3239521.003.105.

Ong, Walter. "The Writer's Audience Is Always Fiction." *PMLA*, vol. 90, no. 1, 1975, pp. 9–21.

Osborne Randall E., et al. "Student Effects of Service–Learning: Tracking Change across a Semester." *Michigan Journal of Community Service Learning*, vol. 5, no. 1, 1998, pp. 5–13, http://hdl.handle.net/2027/spo.3239521.0005.101.

Park, Douglas B. "Analyzing Audiences." *College Composition and Communication*, vol. 37, no. 4, Dec. 1986, pp. 478–88.

—. "The Meanings of 'Audience.'" *College English*, vol. 44, no. 3, Mar. 1982, pp. 247–57.

Pinkert, Laurie A., and Kendall Leon. "Heuristic Tracing and Habits for Learning: Developing Generative Strategies for Understanding Service Learning." *Reflections: A Journal of Community–Engaged Writing and Rhetoric*, vol. 19, no. 2, Fall/Winter 2019–2020, pp. 36–85, https://reflectionsjournal.net/wp-content/uploads/2020/03/V19.N2.Pinkert.pdf.

Rafoth, Bennett A. "Audience and Information." *Research in the Teaching of English*, vol. 23, no. 3, 1989, pp. 273–90.

Reid, Joy, and Barbara Kroll. "Designing and Assessing Effective Classroom Writing Assignments for NES and ESL Students." *Journal of Second Language Writing*, vol. 4, no. 1, 1995, pp. 17–41.

Reiff, Mary Jo. "Rereading 'Invoked' and 'Addressed' Readers Through a Social Lens: Toward a Recognition of Multiple Audiences." *JAC: A Journal of Composition Theory*, vol. 16, no. 3, 1996, pp. 407–24.

Roozen, Kevin. "Writing Is a Social and Rhetorical Activity." *Naming What We Know: Threshold Concepts of Writing Studies*, edited by Linda Adler–Kassner and Elizabeth A. Wardle, Utah State U P, 2015, pp. 17–19.

Rosinski, Paula, and Tim Peeples. "Forging Rhetorical Subjects: Problem–Based Learning in the Writing Classroom." *Composition Studies*, vol. 40, no. 2, 2012, pp. 9–33, https://compositionstudiesjournal.files.wordpress.com/2019/01/cs40n2-fall2012.pdf.

Tracy, Sarah J. *Qualitative Research Methods: Collecting Evidence, Crafting Analysis, Communicating Impact*, Wiley–Blackwell, 2013.

Trimbur, John. "Composition and the Circulation of Writing." *College Composition and Communication*, vol. 52, no. 2, 2000, pp. 188–219.

van Manen, Max. *Researching Lived Experience: Human Science for an Action Sensitive Pedagogy*. Second Edition, Routledge, 2016.

Warner, Michael. "Introduction: Fear of a Queer Planet." *Social Text*, no. 29, 1991, pp. 3–17.

Wurr, Adrian J. "Text–Based Measures of Service–Learning Writing Quality." *Writing and Community Engagement: A Critical Sourcebook*, edited by Thomas Deans et al., Bedford/St. Martin's, 2010, pp. 422–34.

Learning Institutional Ecologies for Inventive Collaboration in Writing Center/Classroom Collaboration

Elizabeth Maffetone and Rachel McCabe

This article explores how knowledge of institutional ecologies can help build connections across departments of large universities without direct communication. The authors, an instructor and a writing center tutor, consider "inventive collaboration"—impromptu work mediated by student writing—as a way to improve a multilingual student's writing. This experience serves as a test case to highlight how the rhetorical strategies of inventive collaboration can improve students' rhetorical attunement, awareness of audience, and agency over their writing. While the authors recognize the uniqueness of their indirect collaboration, they also offer an assessment of the institutional and individual components that allowed for this collaboration to take place.

In the spring of 2016, Rachel McCabe and Elizabeth Maffetone developed an unexpected and unplanned collaboration over student work. This collaboration took place at a large public midwestern institution, Indiana University Bloomington (IU), and connected the university's separate writing center and English department, where the writing program is located. Rachel was a graduate instructor of a first year multilingual composition course, and Elizabeth was a graduate student tutor in the university writing center.[1] Building on what William Duffy defines as an interactionist, object-oriented frame for collaboration theory, we outline in this article what we have termed an "inventive collaboration" that allowed us—and our student—to navigate some of the systemic issues of authority between the classroom and the writing center. Inventive collaboration, as we define it here, is a stance towards working together mediated by students and student texts. It takes as its premise that knowledge of institutional ecologies allows students, faculty, and staff to articulate their place in universities in ways that makes their collective work more productive and can better support student writers.

Our collaboration hinged on two factors: our shared composition training, which stressed our location within the university's ecological network, and our mutual investment in putting student learning and agency before personal authority. Our inventive collaboration demonstrates the importance of learning about institutional ecologies, particularly in spaces where direct collaboration is not accessible. While the congenial relationship between the university's writing program and writing center laid the groundwork for our collaboration, the flexibility of this model demonstrates the potential for inventive collaborations to support Writing Program Administrators (WPAs) and Writing Center Directors (WCDs) within university networks more broadly. Inventive collaboration can bridge the gap between WPAs and WCDs, which more often serve as separate entities than as integrated pieces of the student writing process.

Framing Institutional Structures and Collaborative Models

Despite their shared goals and approaches, collaborations between writing centers and writing programs are not as common or easy as one might hope or assume. Linda S. Bergmann explains that writing centers often make considerable contact with people across campus and divisions—in part because of their reputation for being the "go-to" place for writing help. Despite this reputation, Bergmann explains that writing centers are often marginalized by the larger academic community because their work is, at times, removed from the day-to-day work of academic instructors (no courses, no grading, etc.).[2] We argue that one way such divides might be bridged is through a greater understanding of institutional ecologies—the scope, role, and intersections among different campus entities.

The importance of ecological impacts on student writing has been a subject of composition scholarship for decades. Marilyn Cooper's 1986 article "The Ecology of Writing" examines how student writers and their work "… both determine and are determined by the characteristics of all the other writers and writings in the systems" (Cooper 368). This constant influence from the many members of the larger writing community results in ecologies that are "inherently dynamic; though their structures and contents can be specified at a given moment, in real time they are constantly changing, limited only by parameters that are themselves subject to change over longer spans of time" (Cooper 368). The constant changes of, and within, these learning ecologies highlight how different practices within organizations can have different impacts on individual writers, and why communication within any organization is so vital. In addition, acknowledging the presence of ecologies of writing allows for easier navigation among them. Using universal language and avoiding jargon, acknowledging common goals across different university systems, employing ethnographic thinking, and remaining open-minded to the different practices within other parts of the university are all critical in maintaining unity across different ecologies.[3]

Cooper advocates an ecological model of writing because it moves beyond the individual writer to consider the way "writers interact to form systems" and, as a result, form and are formed by the writers and writings within these systems (368). Cooper argues that at its most ideal, the ecological model projects "an infinitely extended group of people who interact through writing, who are connected by the various systems that constitute the activity of writing" (372). Although Cooper's emphasis is primarily on the writer within a system, we see Cooper's model providing a useful way to think about ecologies from the institutional perspective as well, because knowledge of writing ecologies can also become more important as institutional—that is, university—size increases. In the case of the collaborative work between writing centers and writing programs, this means emphasizing the ways each of these different contexts allows students glimpses into different "universities" as they invent them.[4] Not only do students need to learn the expectations of these two parts of the larger institution, but they also need to see these differences not as confusing or upsetting—acknowledging these differences as resulting from the different institutional ecologies at play. As we will show, this can help students to think more rhetorically about the writing process.

Although our work builds heavily from the notion of "institutional ecologies," our practice aligns with a methodological model of thinking described by Michelle LaFrance as institutional ethnography. As she describes it, institutional ethnography offers a model of viewing institutions from one's vantage point within them in order to reveal overlooked everyday experience (4). In practice, this method involves seeing the ways that institutional contexts inflect the work that we do as writers, pedagogues, and workers. LaFrance notes that the field of composition has often theorized the "institutional" as reflecting a greater attention to "broad rhetorical patterns in the field, the university, and higher education *than to the ways individual people actually negotiate those discourses in an everyday sense*" (14). By considering how institutional ecologies directly impacted our relationship to the student in question and how the student interacted with the ecologies in play, we simultaneously investigate the university's ecologies and their impact on individual members of the learning community.

Awareness of Institutional Ecologies: A Reflection on Our Experience

In order to show students the systems in which they are writing, instructors must be aware of those systems. While our training did not explicitly use the terminology LaFrance employs, her discussion of the virtues of institutional ethnography and its ability to help workers within institutions see how those institutions shape individuals' attitudes, was foundational in our training at IU. The success of our collaborative relationship was cultivated primarily by our deep understanding of our roles and positions in larger institutional ecologies. There were a number of unique factors that contributed to this understanding, but foremost was our shared training: we had both been trained as instructors within the English department, under the supervision of Dana Anderson, the Director of Composition.[5] Our initial programmatic training involved a week-long orientation at the start of the fall semester and a semester-long pedagogical theory course that includes supplemental practical support intended to prepare instructors to teach first year composition.[6]

A key component of this training had been to invite and include members of organizations and departments across the university to introduce themselves and the different resources available to instructors and students. These guests ranged from administrators and experienced instructors within the department to representatives from campus-wide resources such as Title IX and the campus writing center.[7] In addition to these formal presentations, the Director of Composition also devoted a session of the Proseminar[8] to outlining where the first year composition course fits within the larger institutional structure as well as the curricular objectives and where those objectives come from: the state, the university, the department, and the CWPA Outcomes for First Year Writing. By showcasing the many parts of the institution with which the writing program remains in conversation, we were invited to see Rachel's work in the classroom and Elizabeth's work in the writing center, not as isolated spaces of learning, but as one place of many where students work to improve their communication skills. Moreover, the emphasis on the way the different programs work to serve larger institutional, state, and national aims allowed us to articulate the shared goals and objectives of our individual work. As a result, our training helped us recognize the importance and difference of the work within both the classroom and the tutorial space well before our collaboration began.

Case Study

Our paths first crossed in 2016, when Rachel was teaching multilingual composition and Elizabeth was working as a tutor in the university's writing center. At the beginning of the semester, Rachel alerted students to the different resources available to them, including instructor office hours and the tutoring sessions available at the writing center. As the semester progressed, many students attended office hours, and some brought drafts of their work that had clearly received input from the writing center. One student in particular made a point to meet with Rachel at least once a week and informed her that he had a weekly appointment with the writing center as well. The student with whom we worked, like many of his classmates, was very interested in figuring out what his instructor wanted for each writing assignment and was often very frustrated when Rachel asked more questions than she provided answers. A normal meeting consisted of him repeatedly asking if his choices were correct and Rachel asking him about the rhetorical goals of his writing.

Elizabeth's relationship with the student began when he brought his first assignment, a summary, into the writing center to be tutored. The student's goals for the tutorial were focused on grades and grammar, an approach we might expect given Carol Severino's work on student perceptions of tutoring. However, it quickly became clear that his first assignment had been inadvertently plagiarized. Elizabeth asked the student to explain his choices and why they were appropriate for his audience; however, the student insisted he had included those points and passages because "they are there." When Elizabeth asked the student to show her "where" exactly "there" was, the student pulled up a webpage with a summary of the text in question and she realized that the student had copy-pasted the summary into theirs. Through this discovery, Elizabeth shifted into a more directive tutoring style, explaining that copying a summary from the internet constituted plagiarism. The student was daunted by the prospect of having to rewrite the paper and, in response, Elizabeth leveraged the student's focus on his grade and awareness of the instructor as audience. She explained that if he did not rewrite the paper, he would fail the assignment; she explained that Rachel would certainly give the student a "Zero-F." To avoid such possible consequences, Elizabeth encouraged the student to begin his draft anew. During the remainder of the tutorial, the student and Elizabeth worked through the text to be summarized, and she helped him build a summary in his own words. While the student was concerned with what he perceived as the inelegance of his language, Elizabeth consistently underscored that ownership of his work was what mattered most. When he attributed the positive result of his first paper to his tutor, she reminded him that *he* wrote the paper and it was *his words* that earned him the high grade; she had merely caught an error before it became unfixable.

Meanwhile, in office hours, Rachel continually asked the student what direction *he* wanted to take his writing, since there was no "right answer" to each assignment. When he brought up ideas Elizabeth had suggested, particularly when they may have conflicted with advice Rachel was providing, she reiterated that while multiple successful avenues were possible, the student needed to choose which option he felt was most conducive to his rhetorical goal. The student's recognition of the rhetorical attunement Elizabeth developed as a tutor meant that he was inclined to share the comments he had received from Rachel in office, partly because he wanted her input on how to address them. Both tutor and instructor saw their role as helping the student navigate the expectations of different academic audiences in order to best support the argument he wanted to make.

Though the student had brought feedback from Rachel (the things he wanted to "fix") into the tutorial, Elizabeth emphasized these comments as suggestions and jumping-off points to help the student arrive at his own ideas. When the student expressed anxiety about comments that he felt were not addressed in the tutorial or were in conflict with one another, Elizabeth encouraged him to go to office hours, to show Rachel his draft, and to discuss further steps for revision; Elizabeth also encouraged him to explain to Rachel why he took a different tack to his paper. Meanwhile, as Rachel's meetings with the student continued, he began articulating his learning in tutorial and similarly questioning if suggestions were right or if he was on the right track. He was particularly concerned when the tutor and instructor input differed, and Rachel's word choice in these situations was very specific: she explained that there were multiple ways to execute the different goals of his writing, and that it was up to him to choose which option was most successful based on *his* goals. In moments where the student might question a comment Rachel made if it conflicted with Elizabeth's, Elizabeth would reinforce Rachel's authority and expertise, noting that Rachel, as the instructor, may have different priorities than Elizabeth did, and that the best course of action would be to speak further with her about such conflicts. Similarly, Rachel did not use office hours as a space to dismiss or reject Elizabeth's feedback as a tutor. Instead, she regularly explained to the student that what he perceived as conflicts were really multiple approaches to the same goal and placed the decision-making authority onto the student: as the writer, it was up to him to choose the approach that would be most fruitful based on his own priorities and goals for his work.

This became the norm of our working relationship: we would dialogue individually with the student, acting as sounding-boards for ideas and providing suggestions where appropriate. The student's shared notes would then become a shared text across meetings. Through this exchange, we came to develop a deeply collaborative relationship with each other through this student. As the semester progressed and the student became more confident in his writing and language skills, our tutorials moved toward collaboration.

This resulted in two important outcomes: first, the tutorial developed into a semester-long relationship, not just between the student and Elizabeth, but between the tutor and instructor (despite not knowing one another or contacting one another directly), mediated by student writing; second, the student began to focus and develop his own rhetorical agency over his own writing. For example, in one instance when he and Rachel discussed the rationale for Elizabeth's suggestion, he noted, "This is my paper, so I'll think about it and decide." This moment showed us that this student had finally gained the confidence to prioritize what we had throughout our work with him: his own voice. This was the crux of our inventive collaboration across institutional ecologies.

Our inventive collaboration also helped ameliorate many traditional expectations associated with top-down program and placement models. As Candace Spigelman reminds us "Composition theory makes us aware that literacy practices are never ideologically neutral" (39). In particular, the labels used within the institution can have a significant impact on student understanding of their place in the university. Spigelman explains, "Beyond the conflict of student power relations, beyond the possibility that students can ever be 'written' as something more or less than 'student' is the question of how labels like 'basic writer' and 'peer group leader' construct student identities" (Spigelman 39). Much like the "basic" label, multilingual students are often labeled as "other" to the university's writing programming. This othering can lead many to assume that they are in need of remedial help. For this reason, "tutorial" services are often interpreted as remedial support for students who need additional help with their writing.

This is part of the reason that a knowledge of institutional ecologies can be particularly fruitful for tutors and instructors working with multilingual students. It allows instructors to view writing centers, and the work they do, not as remedial but as an important part of a larger ecology; as a result, this knowledge may mitigate the "othering" multilingual students may feel in approaching writing centers for assistance. In the case of our student, these ideas about writing centers as remedial were deeply ingrained. Although Rachel had stressed the importance of the writing center to writers of all skill levels, he nonetheless entered the writing center with a fix-it approach to the work that the center did, as well as a sense that he had been sent there for language-based remediation.

However, through the rigorous work he encountered in the center, the exchanges among the three of us, and our consistent reference and attention to larger institutional ecologies, the student came to understand the different roles and goals of the classroom, office hours, and writing center. The student came to see all these spaces as part of a larger ecology working to develop him as a writer, and he began to view himself as a kind of "insider" rather than outsider. He came to realize the ways in which writing is rarely done in isolation; it is often a conversation and, more than that, it is often collaborative. The student continued to come to the writing center long after he had mastered the skills he had initially sought to learn from us. This was largely due to his increased sense of himself as writing for, and with, other writers in an institutional ecology.

Analysis of Our Inventive Collaboration

In our analysis of this case study, we have concluded that our awareness of the university's ecologies had a twofold effect. First, it encouraged both of us to err on the side of trust and generosity. Although we were both already inclined towards trust and generosity, our program's emphasis on the ways larger institutional ecologies speak to one another allowed us to leverage this trust into a transformative collaborative relationship. In addition, Elizabeth's work (and earlier training) within the English Department and Rachel's understanding of the writing center's responsibilities and values allowed for a deepening of our trust and respect: we both knew that we were operating from a shared mission and, importantly, understood the ways our work was both distinct from each other and integral to developing student writers. This not only paved the way for productive work with the student, but it also highlighted for the student how his work could function as both product and process in these larger institutional ecologies.

While many of the collaborations explored in Alice Johnson Myatt and Lynée Lewis Gaillet's *Writing Program and Writing Center Collaborations* stress strategies developed directly between WCD and WPA, the size and structure of IU, in addition to the strict privacy requirements of IU's Writing Center, meant that direct collaboration (except under very specific circumstances) was difficult or prohibited.[9] Instead, knowledge of the different parts of student writing support came from training: the early introduction between new writing instructors and the university's WCD, as well as reminders of the university's resources during Proseminar.

Our knowledge of institutional ecologies not only structured our collaborative endeavor, influencing the collective work we were doing with the student, but it also made the process more egalitarian in general. In "Tutoring and Teaching: Continuum, Dichotomy, or Dialectic?" Helon Howell Raines explores the possible missteps that can occur when the classroom and writing center are "points on a continuum" which makes both spaces so similar they ultimately begin to compete—or are dichotomous—which makes writing centers subservient to the classroom (Raines 153). Instead of these, she proposes "a dialectical view, more specifically the Hegelian dialectical process, in which opposing forces conflict, but in their meeting they also mix, each altering the other until ultimately both transcend the interaction to become something new" (Raines 153). This dialectic avoids some of the identity issues with the top-down model in place when the classroom dictates the work done in tutorial (Carino 112). Raines also suggests that this model more naturally mimics the reality of the classroom/tutorial relationship and it therefore "reflects a desirable process that avoids privileging any particular position except in the situational context. The expectation of interplay between the activities should encourage difference without seeking domination" (157). According to Raines, however, this requires difficult work: "more productive conversation could result when teachers and tutors have clearer concepts of what each does, why, where their roles overlap, converge, or blend, and how they can more positively reinforce one another" (150). Our example demonstrates the ecological approach to doing such work: inventive collaboration organically developed as our student utilized both of us as resources, an especially important dialectic at larger institutions where these departments often remain separate or separated.

Subversive Measures toward Inventive Collaboration: Metaphors and Mediated Conversation

As we have emphasized, our shared knowledge of institutional ecologies was a large influence in the development of this collaboration. However, our knowledge of ecologies does not fully explain the success of this inventive collaboration for the student, nor does it fully account for its dynamics. Collaboration, in Andrea Lunsford's words, is "damnably difficult," blossoming, as it sometimes does, against "The students', tutors', and teachers' prior experiences; … the school day and term; and the drop-in nature of many centers" (6). Raines's and Lunsford's arguments highlight that true collaboration is often elusive, even when all parties approach the process with the best of intentions.

In addition, work in composition tends to collapse collaboration and "conversation," the latter often described as a back-and-forth exchange between its interlocutors. One primary site for this collapsing is the "Burkean Parlor" metaphor, a model of student writing that suggests writing center work is intended to help students think about their place in the conversation about writing: a conversation is already occurring, and they enter into it, adding their voice and guiding it in such a way that multiple perspectives are heard, to produce a nuanced conversation. Lunsford calls for the writing center to adopt this Burkean Parlor method to stress the collaboration of multiple voices, and recent scholarship has continued to express interest in this model and call for an expansion of its definition (Walsh et al.).

Although some scholars have pushed back against the connections of conversation and collaboration (Duffy), what undergirds normative definitions of conversation and collaboration are assumptions of space, place, and time. During an interview, Lisa Ede and Andrea Lunsford quip about finding collaborators through a "Collaborative Writing Dating Service" (12). Their statement underscores, even in jest, the assumption that collaboration is an intimate activity that includes—if not demands—direct contact (see also: Myatt). However, during the entire semester that we collaboratively worked with this student, we never spoke directly and, in fact, did not really know one another. Rather, our collaboration occurred in a third space: the student's writing.[10] Not only did the student vocalize the ideas of each of us to the other, but we also had a loose transcript of the events in each person's meeting because we were both helping the student draft an action plan for future work in each meeting. This distance, contrary to popular belief, seemed to actually help rather than hinder our collaboration. Because of the writing center's strict confidentiality policy, all contact between us was filtered through the student. As a rule, this meant that the student needed to choose whether and what about our meetings he would convey to the other. This also meant that our work was, by necessity, focused on the student's aims and goals as he framed our (limited) interactions with one another. In this case, our lack of direct communication placed the student at the center of the collaboration and ensured valuing of his voice.

So, although composition and writing center scholarship often uses "conversation" as both metaphor and practice, inventive collaboration of the kind we experienced does not require direct exchange between interlocutors. Indeed, it does not require collaborators to be in contact at all. Instead, inventive collaboration promotes a working together through shared senses of institutional ecology in a way mediated by student texts and motivated by a shared openness toward supporting student writers.

In addition, our inventive collaboration depended on mutual openness toward the other party's influence on the student's writing. In the process, our teamwork challenged traditional ideas about our roles as instructor and tutor. As defined by Lunsford and Ede in a 1991 interview, the collaborative model of writing challenges the traditional classroom model. According to Lunsford, "collaboration is subversive because it challenges notions of individual authorship and responsibility for an autonomous text. We know also that it challenges our whole system of testing, measurement, and evaluation and that it questions the way we, as teachers, respond to and assess our students" (*Writing on the Edge* 18). In our inventive collaborative model, this subversion was clear in both office hours and tutorial sessions: the student was encouraged to consider the ways both support systems shaped his writing while deciding which suggestions were important to his writing and which were not. His mediation of the inventive collaboration made it such that both Rachel's and Elizabeth's commitment to the student's writing process took precedence over any individual investment. Instead, the student's understanding of each contributor was the constant focus.

In addition to the respect instilled by the Proseminar we both attended, mutual generosity was also key to the success of this inventive collaboration. In our experience, during both office hours and tutorial sessions, students occasionally juxtapose the feedback from their instructor or tutor when they see a discrepancy between the two types of input they're receiving. We have both found that these moments are more often a result of the student learning to process feedback and recalibrate throughout the writing process than they are an attempt to undermine the authority or input of their instructors or tutors. In these cases generally, and this case study specifically, our generosity toward the suggestions of instructor and tutor, along with flexibility in understanding as the student mediated our input, led to a stance of conversational openness that allowed for the success of this model.

Despite the challenges to organic collaboration, the progress our student made during the course of the semester seems to be indicative of what inventive collaboration between the writing center and the first year writing classroom can achieve. This collaboration brought to the fore what these spaces purport to do at their best: giving students the tools they need to succeed in college-level writing. Elizabeth Busekru explains that "as the student develops a writing voice and explores more than one angle on a topic and/or within a discipline, this student takes a side regarding what to believe" (12). The kairotic potential of a composing moment, as Busekrus points out, brings more options than a "conversation" might initially suggest, and as a result, "[t]his collaborative environment signifies resistance because other perspectives are brought to attention" (12). In effect, then, inventive collaboration stages the "resistance … of other perspectives" by 1) emerging from knowledge about institutional ecologies toward 2) a somewhat subversive approach to both collaboration and conversation via the mediation of student texts, and 3) undergirding that subversion through openness to multiple perspectives and a disposition of respect and generosity toward those perspectives. The success of such inventive collaboration, of course, rests on the response of the student to the tension between perspectives, and the student's willingness to enact agency and exercise authority over their text.

Collaboration's Impact for Student Learners: Student Agency and Rhetorical Attunement

For multilingual students in particular, the different levels of institutional authority can be challenging to navigate, particularly between the classroom and writing center. As Spigelman explains regarding student/teacher power relations, "problems of hierarchy and power cannot be attributed merely to students' predilections or even to their academic insecurity. Power relations are a significant and inevitable feature of every teacher-student engagement, even for those of us who would have it be otherwise" (Spigelman 43). Neither are power dynamics between teacher and student wholly interpersonal: institutional ecologies influence how each views the other. These difficulties are further complicated when students have multicultural understandings of their own writing and learning processes.

In our experience, multilingual students often have a complex relationship to the model of authority present in the writing center. Some students see the writing center as a punishment; others see tutors as employees whose job it is to improve student grammar. Many multilingual students approach the writing center with a particular kind of rhetorical attunement, "an emergent sensitivity to language and borrows from these tuning metaphors the honed quality of multilingual sensibilities, as isolated literate moments are situated in the context of changing global conditions" (Leonard 230). Thus, multilingual students are often hyper-aware of the need for language to fit a particular audience or context, and they seek out assistance in meeting this goal. In the case of our student, this manifested itself in two ways: 1) the initial reason the student reached out to us in the first place, and 2) the student's anxiety over negotiating our expectations, especially conflicting feedback.

The mediated conversation employed by our inventive collaboration was particularly successful because it allowed both of us to draw on and develop the student's pre-existing rhetorical awareness. Despite the student's initial focus on grades and his relationship to a "right answer," we mutually reinforced that he was the author of his writing and that no single choice would lead to a better grade. In response, the student re-tuned his sensitivity to focus on how choices worked well for the goal he articulated for his essays. This reattunement moved the student writer toward what Canagarajah expresses as the two central goals for multilingual writing practice: 1) awareness that difference does not necessarily equate to error, and 2) the writing process is a performance and should not be confined to "text production" (603). This shift was critical for our multilingual writer because many of the assumptions he made about his work came from a binary understanding of rhetorical choices: they are either right or wrong. Our inventive collaboration helped him see that he had choices and control over his writing and the potential results of his choices. This "context-transforming" work, as Canagarajah explains, helps student writers understand that "Texts are not simply context-bound or context-sensitive" and that "students should not treat rules and conventions as given or pre-defined for specific texts and contexts." (603). Inventive collaboration, then, shows that instructors and tutors are "developing not only competent writers, but also critical writers" (Canagarajah 603). Through our mutual reinforcement of the student's autonomy in his writing choices, we helped the student build his already strong rhetorical awareness into his writing.

In addition, rhetorical attunement can support multilingual students in drawing connections regarding the power of language, as it "highlights the rhetorical in multilingualism: its instability and contingency, its political weight and contextual embeddedness. In fact, calling attunement rhetorical serves to underline these elements—materiality, contingency, emergence, resistance" (Leonard 230). This rhetorical attunement, then, can be potentially beneficial. It can allow the student flexibility and awareness of their audience. More, it can lead the student to reflect on their grade merely as feedback from their audience, since they are attuned to the ways in which the rhetorical situation changes depending on the instructor's choices for the assignment. Remember:

the student and Elizabeth's relationship developed because she managed to catch his plagiarism. The outcome of that interaction demonstrates how the recognition and strategic awareness of audience can set the stage for collaborative work between tutors and students. Elizabeth relied on her rhetorical proficiency as a tutor and instructor to tell the student exactly what needed to be done (rewrite the paper) and to position herself as "a nonjudgmental, non-evaluative helper" (Harris 376).

Elizabeth and Rachel also both routinely conferred authority over the student's writing back to the student. During this semester-long process, the student listened to the guidance provided by the instructor and tutor, ultimately choosing which options were most effective for him based on his own rhetorical understanding of his writing process. We did not view our authority as being in competition with one another; rather, we loaned our authority to the student and to each other. Our collaboration hinged on recognizing our positions of authority and using them to help the student build confidence in his authorial voice; we moved the student's focus on finding "right" answers to finding the most accurate way *he* wanted to express his ideas.

Rhetorical attunement and agency were the primary aims and outcomes of our collaboration with each other and this student. As we emphasized our own roles in the larger institutional ecologies, and our shared values, the student came to view his work as being a part of that larger ecology. That is, while neither of us shirked the responsibility of our institutional positions, we also reminded the student that there was not necessarily a "right" or "wrong" approach, but rather that different audiences have different expectations and that every writer must navigate those expectations. Over time, the student's voice became the most dominant one in his writing.

Conclusion

Our example stresses the need for, and potential success of, a more inventive model of collaboration built from knowledge of institutional ecologies. We worked together for the benefit of the student, placing his sense of agency and developing voice at the forefront of our common goal. While we understand that this is always the expectation, that instructors and tutors are always supposed to be working to support student writers, we also acknowledge the limitations set in place by institutional hierarchies, personal investment in program models, and the lack of resources (particularly time) available for developing direct lines of collaboration. That said, training that stresses knowledge of ecologies helps facilitate the potential for these inventive collaborations. Because Indiana University's training introduced writing instructors to their location within a network of student writing support, Rachel was aware of the benefits of the writing center and encouraged students to visit as a resource. Similarly, Elizabeth's awareness (as both instructor and tutor) of the mission and values of the university's first year writing program helped facilitate continuity of feedback in her work with students. When this background was combined with our mutual investment in student agency and voice, the organic dialogue that developed within, and on, his writing, we produced an inventive collaboration. In turn, this collaboration produced student-centered instruction. In particular, our collaboration shows the ways in which an awareness of larger campus offices—especially their institutional role and purpose—might facilitate moments of inventive collaboration.

This experience shaped our time as assistant directors of first year writing, a role we would both accept two years after our inventive collaboration. During this work we realized the impact of our early exchange and were able to continue to stress the importance of the ecologies of the university to new composition instructors. This experience also helped us make changes to the relationship between the writing center and first year writing programs. In our training process for new instructors, we expanded and reframed the role of the writing center; rather than offering a brief presentation and overview, the writing center offered a tutoring demo, which we paired with readings about office hours and tutorial philosophy. As a result, instructors were offered more than a glimpse into what the writing center had to offer; instructors also saw the tutors in the writing center as experts at conferencing with and developing student writers.

Additionally, our teaching stressed the value of flexibility and generosity to new instructors. In describing the benefits of our inventive collaboration to them, we showcased the possible benefits of openness toward other aspects of the university's support system for students. On many occasions, we were able to reframe communication from other instructors and administrators in terms of their investment and concern for student well-being, which is often at the heart of so many moments of communication across departments. While we don't expect that every composition instructor will have an experience as directly influential on student writing as ours, openness to the possibility models the ways future instructors and tutors can make room for inventive collaboration as a way to support multilingual student writers.

Notes

1. FYC and the WC at Indiana University Bloomington exist in different parts of the university and each program had a separate training process. As a result, both parts of the university were able to acknowledge the importance of one another, but there was little cross-over in personnel.

2. Concerns about marginalization are echoed in Anne Ellen Geller and Harry Denny's "Of Ladybugs, Low Status, and Loving the Job: Writing Center Profession-

als Navigating Their Careers." In their study of Writing Center Professionals, they noted that while WCPs tend to be satisfied with their work some expressed feeling like oddities in their institutions or home departments and others noted the difficulty having their writing center work counted towards tenure (106-107).

3. In *Institutional Ethnography: A Theory of Practice for Writing Studies* Michelle LaFrance discusses how ethnographic thinking, and its use within writing programs, can be used to better understand the ways individuals operate within institutions.

4. While David Bartholomae's "Inventing the University" stresses the difficulty of learning the expectations of different types of writing within the university, we stress the importance of acknowledging these different "universities" within the larger writing experience and the benefits of being open to these differences.

5. Anderson was director of Composition from 2010 through 2018. In addition to training us both as graduate students, we also worked with him as Assistant Directors of the Composition Program from 2017-2019.

6. This course acted, in some ways, as what LaFrance might term a "boss text"; that is, a way of creating ideals of accountability and professionalization (43). As she notes, these "boss texts" are not just sources of information but "shapers of thinking and practice" (43).

7. More, the Director of Composition also leads a session for the writing centers' training that generally takes the form of a larger conversation about the related, but distinct, roles both WTS and FYW play in developing student writers. When we became Assistant Directors, these were aspects of the program that we expanded, including a formal tutorial demonstration that coincided with the pedagogical theory course's discussion of conferencing with students.

8. Proseminar was the semester-long course required for all first-time instructors of Composition within IU's English Department. The course included pedagogy workshops, readings on the teaching of college writing, and instructor demonstrations on core concepts of first year writing. The writing program, and the instructor support mechanisms within it, were awarded the 2019 CCCC certificate of excellence.

9. A lack of communication between writing centers and writing programs at large universities is not inevitable. Miley and Downs describe WPAs and WCDs can develop relationships and their programs side by side. For an overview of debates on student privacy and disclosure in writing centers, see: Pemberton; Cogie; and Cordaro.

10. This is not the evaluative third space described by Alyssa-Rae Hug, nor was it (primarily) a conversation between instructor and tutor, rather it was a conversation mediated by the student about his purpose, audience, and authority.

Works Cited

Bartholomae, David. "Inventing the University." *Journal of Basic Writing*, vol. 5, no. 1, 1986, pp. 4–23.

Bergmann, Linda S. "The Writing Center as a Site of Engagement." *Going Public: What Writing Programs Learn from Engagement,* edited by Shirley K Rose and Irwin Weiser. Utah State UP, 2010, pp. 160–76

Busekrus, Elizabeth. "Kairotic Situations: A Spatial Rethinking of the Burkean Parlor in the Writing Center." *Praxis: A Writing Center Journal,* vol. 17, issue 2, 2017, pp. 15–20.

Carino, Peter. "Early Writing Centers: Toward a History," *The Writing Center Journal,* vol. 15, no. 2, 1995, pp. 103–15.

Canagarajah, A. Suresh. "Toward a Writing Pedagogy of Shuttling between Languages: Learning from Multilingual Writers." *College English,* vol. 68, no. 6, 2006, pp. 589-604.

Cogie, Jane. "In Defense of Conference Summaries: Widening the Reach of Writing Center Work." *Writing Center Journal,* vol. 18, no. 2, 1998, pp. 47-70.

Cooper, Marilyn. "The Ecology of Writing." *College English,* vol. 48, no. 4, 1986, pp. 364–75.

Cordaro, Danielle. "Practical Uses for Session Reports Among Faculty: A Case Study." *The Writing Lab Newsletter,* vol. 38, no. 9-10, 2014, pp. 1-6.

Duffy, William. "Collaboration (in) Theory: Reworking the Social Turn's Conversational Imperative." *College Englis*h, vol. 76, no. 5, 2014, pp. 416–35.

Geller, Anne Ellen and Harry Denny. "Of Ladybugs, Low Status, and Loving the Job: Writing Center Professionals Navigating Their Careers." *The Writing Center Journal,* vol. 33, no. 1, 2013, pp. 96–129.

Harris, Muriel. "Collaboration Is Not Collaboration Is Not Collaboration: Writing Center Tutorials vs. Peer-Response Groups." *College Composition and Communication,* vol. 43, no. 3, 1992, pp. 369–83.

Heim, Alice, et al. "An Interview with Andrea Lunsford and Lisa Ede: Collaboration as a Subversive Activity." *Writing on the Edge,* vol. 2, no. 2, 2001, pp. 7–18.

Hug, Alyssa-Rae. "Two's Company, Three's a Conversation: A Study of Dialogue among a Professor, a Peer-Writing Fellow, and Undergraduates around Feedback and Writing." *Praxis,* vol. 11 no. 1, 2013, pp. 1–7.

LaFrance, Michelle. *Institutional Ethnography.* Utah State UP, 2019.

Leonard, Rebecca Lorimer. "Multilingual Writing as Rhetorical Attunement." *College English,* vol. 76, no. 3, 2014, pp. 227–47.

Lunsford, Andrea. "Collaboration, Control, and the Idea of a Writing Center." *The Writing Center Journal,* vol. 12, no. 1, 1991, pp. 3–10.

Lunsford, Andrea A. and Lisa Ede. "Reflection on Contemporary Currents in Writing Center Work." *The Writing Center Journal,* vol. 31, no. 1, 2011, pp. 11–24.

Miley, Michelle and Doug Downs. "Crafting Collaboricity: Harmonizing the Force Fields of Writing Program and Writing Center Work." *Writing Program and Writing Center Collaborations,* edited by Alice Johnston and Lynée Lewis Gaillet. Palgrave Macmillan, 2017, pp. 24–45.

Myatt, Alice Johnston, and Lynée Lewis Gaillet. *Writing Program and Writing Center Collaborations.* Palgrave Macmillan, 2017.

Pemberton, Michael A. "Writing Center Ethics: Sharers and Seclusionists." *Writing Lab Newsletter,* vol. 20, no. 3, 1995, pp. 13–14.

Raines, Helon Howell. "Tutoring and Teaching: Continuum, Dichotomy, or Dialectic?" *The Writing Center Journal,* vol. 14, no. 2, 1994, pp. 150–62.

Salem, Lori. "Decisions . . . Decisions: Who Chooses to Use the Writing Center?" *The Writing Center Journal*, vol. 35, no. 2, 2016, pp. 147–71.

Severino, Carol. "Rhetorically Analyzing Collaboration(s)." *The Writing Center Journal*, vol. 13, no.1, 1992, pp. 53–64.

Spigelman, Candace. "Restructuring Authority: Negotiating Power in Democratic Learning Sites." *Composition Studies*, vol. 29, no. 1, 2001, pp. 27–49.

Walsh, Lynda, Adrian M. Zytkoskee, Patrick Ragains, Heidi Slater, and Michelle Rachal. "The Burkean Parlor as a Boundary Object: A Collaboration between First-Year Writing and the Library." *Composition Studies*, vol. 46, no. 1, 2018, pp. 102–23.

Weisser, Christian R. and Sidney I. Dobrin. "Breaking New Ground in Ecocomposition: An Introduction." *Ecocomposition: Theoretical and Pedagogical Approaches*, edited by Christian R. Weisser and Sidney I. Dobrin, State U of New York P, 2001, pp. 1–10.

Course Design

English 150: Writing as Inquiry—Explorations of Identity and Privilege

Ashanka Kumari and Brita M. Thielen[1]

Course Description

This unit, "Explorations of Identity and Privilege," was designed for first year writing courses at the University of Nebraska-Lincoln (UNL) taught in 2015 and 2016. The course as a whole focused on writing and inquiry. Within this unit, students discussed essays relating to different forms of privilege (e.g. racial, gender, class) and explored their relationship to privilege in a final unit paper. Student writing emphasized self-awareness of how components of their identities—and the identities of others—are rewarded or penalized within their sociocultural environment. While students might be aware of their privilege(s) or lack thereof on some level, reading and discussing essays written by others helped students critically examine their personal experiences within a larger conversation.

Institutional Context

Our experience teaching this unit occurred at UNL, a land-grant institution. The undergraduate community at UNL is overwhelmingly white with the university documenting that in fall 2015, only 13.7% of the undergraduate population was non-white ("Undergraduate Enrollment"). Additionally, the university shows an undergraduate enrollment of roughly 50-55% male to 44-49% female depending on class standing (first year, sophomore, etc.) ("Enrollment"). In 2015, 27% of the entering first year class consisted of first generation students, according to Academic Affairs at UNL. Overall, the majority of students at UNL are from Nebraska, encompassing the more urban communities of Lincoln and Omaha, as well as small farming communities throughout the state. First year students made up the majority of both of our classes with a few sophomores in each section.

Theoretical Rationale

The topic of social privilege[2] is a hot-button issue at many US colleges and universities. Nationwide conversations sparked by the deaths of Trayvon Martin (2012), Eric Garner (2014), Sandra Bland (2015), and the emergence of the #BlackLivesMatter and #SayHerName movements at the time, among others, led us to consider our own privileges. Additionally, social justice concerns related to the distribution of wealth, opportunities, and privileges within society motivated us to design and implement a unit about "Explorations of Identity and Privilege" in our writing classrooms. Such conversations did not seem to happen in our classrooms or, to a degree, on our campus; however, as graduate TAs in our first semesters of teaching in 2015, we also felt unprepared to discuss these incidents directly with our students. We realized that this ability to avoid direct discussions of these incidents was a form of privilege in itself and part of the reason we designed and implemented this unit was to educate ourselves. We hoped to learn alongside our students. Examining issues of identity and privilege allow both students and teachers to contribute to social justice work by unpacking the ways in which individual identities shape access to economic, social, or political power.

Increased attention to the topic of social privilege appears in a variety of departments' course curricula, including psychology (see Boatright-Horowitz et al.; Williams and Malchiori; Platt), sociology (see Messner), ethnic studies, women's, gender, and sexuality studies (see Ferber and O'Reilly Herrera; Case), law (Armstrong and Wildman), cultural studies, and diversity-themed courses (Case and Cole) to name a few, and pedagogical articles on teaching privilege in these disciplines are cropping up with increasing frequency.[3] In composition studies, scholars have written about bringing topics such as difference, whiteness, race, class, gender, and sexuality into the composition classroom (e.g. see Winans; Kynard; Moss; Grobman; Waite). This existing composition scholarship presents the pedagogical affordances to engaging specific identity intersections. Our focus is less on specific facets of identity (e.g. race, class, gender, sexuality) than it is on the relative privileges resulting from an individual's personal identity constellation. Here, our reflections on teaching a unit focused on privilege and identity are informed by these interdisciplinary conversations about privilege and those about intersectionality in composition studies.

A unit on privilege accomplishes several important tasks that forward the development of writers, such as developing research skills, articulating claims, and understanding the rhetorical concepts of audience, purpose, and context. In addition, students practice engaging with and conducting self-reflection and analysis of their own lived experiences in connection with larger social issues through in-class discussions and reflective writing activities. Furthermore, this unit tasks students with fairly and ethically representing themselves and others, as well as developing an awareness of how they present themselves and others as a rhetorical choice.[4] Overall, this unit works to foster habits of mind,[5] particularly curiosity, openness, creativity, responsibility, and metacognition. The writing classroom provides space for students to think critically about their personal interactions with others, the voices they're engaging, and the rhetoric they are surrounded by through the traditional rhetorical triad of audience, purpose, and context.

Our unit particularly fosters openness and responsibility, habits necessary for discussing topics related to social justice. As part of the unit, we present students with the written testimonies of writers whose lived experiences might differ widely from their own in hopes of broadening students' worldviews. We create a classroom environment where students are exposed to the lived experiences of their classmates through the ways we ask students to engage in class discussions and writings. Establishing this environment necessarily supplements the unit's core readings by providing a personal connection to the material. The unit also promotes responsibility by requiring students to think critically about how their everyday actions resonate within their local, national, and even global communities. Not only do students consider how sociocultural forces shape their identities, but they also explore how their actions collectively shape society and culture. This unit fosters critical thinking, or "the ability to analyze a situation or text and make thoughtful decisions based on that analysis" that particularly exposes students to "examining assumptions about the texts [we encounter] held by different audiences" as practiced through a combination of in-class discussions and reflective writing activities ("Framework for Success in Postsecondary Writing").

Critical Reflection

In this critical reflection, we start by first reflecting on our distinct subject positions, which directly impact our varied approaches to teaching this unit. Both of us identify as able-bodied, heterosexual, cisgender women. However, we each hold additional distinguishing identity markers. Specifically, Brita teaches as a white, middle-class, American woman, whereas Ashanka teaches as a first-generation-to-college Indian American woman and child of immigrants. Because her race is embodied through her visible appearance and traditional name, these identity traits are physically revealed to students upon her entrance into her composition classroom. In what follows, we reflect on our individual experiences teaching this unit and key takeaways. We conclude with our collective takeaways and thoughts for how we would retool this unit for future teaching.

Moving Past Single Stories: Ashanka Reflects

By including a unit on privilege in my first year writing class in Spring 2015, I hoped to develop critical awareness alongside students. Specifically, I wanted students to inquire into their own privileges and consider how they manifest regularly in their lives. I also wanted to encourage students to begin to understand how their upbringings, backgrounds, and occupations manifest themselves and to reflect on their ideologies in meaningful ways.

One of the strongest aspects of this unit, and perhaps key, came from introducing these conversations with Chimamanda Adichie's "The Danger of a Single Story." Adichie's talk provided students with vocabulary they could refer back to throughout our discussions such as the concept of a "single story" of a person or group of people, which she argues creates misconceptions when taken as the only story (Adichie). This grounding offered a valuable starting point for forthcoming conversations about representation, writing, and identity. Also, this foregrounding allowed us to have discussions about how to ethically and accurately represent larger cultural and racial communities.

I acknowledged with students that while fairly engaging our own and others' identities can often be challenging, we should approach the unit with honesty and not be afraid to take risks in developing our questions for class discussions and in writing essays for the unit. To offer students a space for taking such risks, I employed the "fishbowl" discussion strategy as a means of creating a lower-stakes environment for a high-stakes discussion by having students work from anonymity to small and large group contexts when sharing their thoughts in response to the core unit texts ("Fishbowl"). In the classroom, I asked students to form a fishbowl space in which four students create a small inner circle of desks with the remaining students in a larger outside circle. Students in the large outside circle are not allowed to speak, following fishbowl rules, unless they are tapped by the facilitator (teacher) or voluntarily tap themselves into the center of the fishbowl to exchange with other students in the center. Through this pedagogical approach, I could gauge students' comprehension of the text and guide the overall discussion as needed, as well as having all students actively participate in both speaking and listening roles. After engaging in the fishbowl and working through several questions for a good part of the class session, I asked students to take a few minutes and write about the questions that remained from those submitted prior to class as well as any concepts that excited or frustrated them from the discussion. Later, in the author's notes accompanying their final unit essays, several students noted that the writing they did during these moments was helpful for drafting the ideas they developed in their projects.

Offering an invitation for students to take risks from the beginning alongside a practice of asking for questions ahead of time helped facilitate discussions of complex topics such as privilege, race, class, and identity. Prior to class, students were asked to read one of the key texts and email questions to me that could foster discussion that I would then compile into a PowerPoint and present without tying any student names to questions to create space for risk taking. For instance, students asked both general questions about terms such as "why [Roxane] Gay feel[s] like everyone needs to accept that they have privilege, and what accepting it would accomplish" to think about the value of such reflection. Or questions about content such as "why Anzaldúa uses a mix of Spanish and English throughout her piece" that opened up conversations about language-use in writing and culture. Students seemed more willing to bring up topics that they might not otherwise for fear or anxiety of how they would be perceived by their peers. Additionally, having students, rather than the teacher, develop the questions for discussion helped ensure the content of the questions was meeting the students' level of understanding and interest. However, this practice took more time in regard to course preparation since I sometimes needed to trim down questions for length or time as well as organize them by topic in the PowerPoint to help the flow of discussion. One thing I would revise in the future is the format and method by which students submit questions. Further, if teaching this three-to-four-week unit as a semester-long theme and/or online, I imagine focusing questions around more specific topics or changing the format would benefit future discussions.

Students did not greet this discussion strategy with open arms. In each class, it seemed the same few students—those who typically participated in every class—would volunteer quickly to be at the center of the fishbowl circle, while others tried to take a spot on the outside of the circle and only participate when called on. However, over time as students got more used to this form, more students would voluntarily tap themselves into the discussion and contribute their feelings on the question at hand. At times, I would mention my personal connections to authors' positions as one way to connect further with students. For instance, while teaching Gloria Anzaldùa's "How to Tame a Wild Tongue," I noted that I grew up in a multilingual household and Anzaldùa's movement among dialects reflected similarly in my household across Hindi, Punjabi, and English. Likewise, I noted that students with shared backgrounds reflected in the readings were likely to volunteer to go first on those particular discussion days. For instance, when we discussed David Sedaris' "Giant Dreams, Midget Abilities," a queer-identified student volunteered to go first; this happened similarly with Latinx-identified students when discussing Anzaldúa. For me, this level of engagement further emphasizes the need for incorporating more intersectional voices in future classrooms—if we only teach white, male authors, for instance, we risk continually privileging, giving agency to, and, thus, often only hearing these voices in the classroom. This discussion model worked to get more conversations happening regarding issues of privilege, race, and identity, but it took a few repetitions of the model before students seemed to feel comfortable participating in speaking roles without my tapping them in.

Overall, the in-class activities along with the readings worked together toward guiding students to transition into brainstorming essay projects. Several students' writing projects stemmed from connections they had written about during in-class fishbowl discussions. The culminating project for this unit was a 6-8 page personal narrative essay. Students were asked to identify and describe a moment or scene that illustrated an example of privilege in their lives, interpret that privilege within a greater context such as their culture, community, or family life, and connect these moments to ideas from one or more of the six key essays taught during this unit. This project blended the concept of the personal narrative essay with critical analysis. I encouraged students to take risks in their writing, as the process of writing drafts with peer review offers opportunities for feedback for students to continue to build their writing. While this project asked students to consider outside voices, the focus of the essay was on the student's narrative with the additional essays serving as support and/or a way to create further points of inquiry into the student's own identities and privileges. Ultimately, students wrote about experiences ranging from growing up as a child of immigrants to how getting a specific tattoo gave her an outsider status within family and home community. The majority of the students in this class pointed to this unit as a moment of both tension and triumph in end-of-semester reflection essays. Specifically, students felt challenged by the texts assigned in the unit, but several noted that this project was among their favorite written pieces because they were able to articulate their concerns and consider what shapes their privileges and identities. Despite limiting the number of readings and scope of the unit, I quickly discovered that the work of this unit could easily encompass an entire course on privilege and identity. When teaching this unit again in the future, I would modify it to include more connections to current events for students to consider alongside our discussions.

Cultivating Compassion and Embracing Vulnerability: Brita Reflects

My primary motivation for teaching a unit on privilege in first year composition was to foster students' compassion for others while developing essential academic writing skills. However, I wanted this compassion to be grounded in critical engagement with the ways in which larger sociocultural systems perpetuate privilege and oppression. In other words, I did not want students' take-away to be merely "feeling badly" about their own social locations, as if issues related to (in)equality are solely within individual control. I speculated that if students were introduced to issues of privilege early in their college careers, they might be open to further engagement as they interact with others and make decisions about future coursework, campus activities, and their future careers. I expected these conversations to be difficult, and I sought to mitigate student resistance by openly acknowledging my own identity markers and privilege and sharing in the vulnerability required by the final essay assignment by composing an essay of my own. Both of these strategies proved effective (as I will demonstrate in the next few paragraphs), although they were not enough to overcome all resistance (as shown in the latter portion of my reflection).

Sharing my identity markers (white, cisgender, heterosexual, middle class, Christian) was beneficial precisely because many of them overlapped greatly with many of the students who attend college in a conservative Midwestern state. Because I made my identity markers visible to them, students realized they could identify with me in many ways, and bringing the topic of privilege to bear on my own life shows students that I am willing to practice what I preach. Furthermore, some combinations of my identity markers can challenge assumptions and binary thinking students might have. For example, I revealed myself to be a practicing Catholic in the same conversation in which I identified as an LGBTQ ally. I shared my religious affiliation with students deliberately, as much of the resistance I experienced when leading this unit at UNL was connected to the strong value many students placed on their Catholic identities. I wanted to show that beliefs and identities at times conflict with one other and that identity is not stable so much as fluid and dynamic. Since the goal of this unit was to encourage students to reflect on key aspects of their identities—and religion deeply influences worldview—I wanted it to be part of the conversation. My religious transparency invited, but did not require, equal transparency from my students, and many students did reflect on the role their religious beliefs played in their lives in discussion and writing activities.[6]

Being open with students about my social location was one way in which I attempted to share vulnerability with students: the other was sharing examples of how I engage with privilege in my own life. I included as a unit text a self-authored creative nonfiction essay centered on my experience of being robbed while serving as a volunteer teacher in Honduras and reflected on the role my privilege played in that event. Sharing this essay helped equalize vulnerability in keeping with bell hooks' warning in *Teaching to Transgress* that "Professors who expect students to share confessional narratives but who are themselves unwilling to share are exercising power in a manner that could be coercive" (21). Before reading my essay, we discussed how their unit papers required engagement with uncomfortable subjects and how I felt it was only fair for me to reciprocate. The class period after reading my essay became an "Ask the Author" session, where we discussed the essay's content and my authorial choices. During this class, students asked a variety of questions regarding the form, content, and research process of my essay, such as "Was this a hard paper for you to write since it was so personal to you? How did you overcome your emotions while writing this essay?" and "While doing research for your paper, did you find a lot of information that you thought would work well in your essay? If so, how did you decide what to include and what to omit?" They also provided thoughtful feedback, including critique.

As I mentioned earlier, however, not every student was willing to engage with the topic of social privilege. Some students openly rejected the idea of privilege in both class discussion and in their low-stakes online writing assignments. For example, I experienced recurring overt resistance from a white male student (referred to here as "David") when I taught this unit in spring 2016. From the start, David was unwilling to acknowledge the existence of privilege and frequently wrote in his discussion board posts that privilege and discrimination did not exist in "the 21st century." In one class, I asked students to describe something they found interesting about an assigned text during a reading quiz. David wrote, "I truthfully learned that people will blame all their own challenges and problems that they made on other things." I later met with David to discuss his resistance to critically engaging with the topic. He was polite and friendly during the meeting as he dismissed his resistance as a simple desire to play "Devil's Advocate." David did not alter his engagement with the topic for the rest of the unit, and his final paper was an examination of his lack of privilege in having divorced parents and his privilege of having a military father (neither of which were aspects of identity that we had been discussing). In retrospect, David's resistance illustrates a significant trade-off for introducing difficult topics such as privilege in the early years of college: students might not yet be emotionally or intellectually mature enough to challenge their pre-existing worldview in any meaningful way. This trade-off does not mean such content should not be taught—just that instructors should acknowledge that they might be unable to work through all resistance. There was one glimmer of success with David, however, as exhibited in his end-of-semester reflection:

> When we started the section that talked about privileges I was totally against it. I felt that it is an old topic that should not be brought up in a class. [...] I mean like I didn't think it existed. I was always brought up that if you wanted to make yourself better in society then you could do so. I have learned in this class that sometimes people have reasons for wanting to study certain areas. I figured out later in the class why you wanted to study privileges. [...] Reading that story [Brita's essay] helped me build great respect for you as a person, and helped me understand exactly what you wanted us to take out of the section. You were not just trying to push the idea of privileges on us (that's what I thought at first) but you were trying to help us understand that it is a real life problem.

David's reaction to my essay seems to support Julie Lindquist's claim that students can benefit from teachers sharing the "affective experience[s] that have produced the teachers' own belief" (191). While shared vulnerability and self-disclosure made David more amenable to the topic of privilege, there are (or should be) limits. Teachers ought to have boundaries with their students, and it is possible for a teacher to cross a line between what is appropriate and inappropriate to share. Student resistance, especially from privileged students, is not something that will disappear. In future classes, it would be important to cultivate methods of engaging resistant students that go beyond instructor self-disclosure.

Collective Takeaways: A Dialogue

The students in our classes approached their final papers in multiple ways. Topics ranged from being a woman in the Lutheran church (religious and gender privileges), to being a bicultural student applying for college scholarships (racial and educational privileges), to experiencing gender discrimination while playing expensive club sports (gender and class privileges), to the benefits of performing traditional and heteronormative masculinity as a male (gender and sexuality privileges), to being a Korean American citizen but not speaking Korean (nationality and linguistic privilege), and to the ability to pursue a college education in another country or state (education and class privileges), among others. The variety of student approaches to the writing project shows the richness the topic of privilege holds for writing that incorporates personal experience, outside research, and cultural and self-analysis. To build on the successful aspects of this unit, we recommend that future iterations take greater advantage of multiple modes of content and delivery, such as incorporating TED Talks, podcasts, and documentaries.

Students also benefit from reading their peers' papers during peer workshops, both in developing their papers as pieces of writing and gaining further insight into the topic of privilege based on each other's personal experiences. Students frequently commented on these benefits from peer workshops in their end-of-unit reflections. Peer workshops are a crucial aspect of this unit's success because it allows students to learn from their peers and realize that many of the issues we touched on in unit readings apply to the lived experiences of people they know.

As we described in our individual sections, one of the biggest hurdles we both experienced when teaching this unit came from student resistance that typically resulted from an inability or unwillingness to move past myths such as meritocracy and a post-racial society that American students have been inculcated with by mainstream American culture for the past several decades. Additionally, the students in our classes (as well as the authors of this article) grew up in so-called colorblind America and were teenagers and young adults during the Obama administration, where discussions of race in white spaces was often either shushed or celebrated as watered-down moments of "multiculturalism" (Armstrong and Wildman 68). This culture, which pervaded our predominantly white classrooms at UNL, made students very uncomfortable thinking about or discussing racism as a continuing problem, as well as resistant to the idea that their whiteness leads to privilege (Armstrong and Wildman 64). Additionally, while they might identify acts of racism on the individual level (Tucker), they are unlikely to see it as a systemic problem. These kinds of reactions were in keeping with "White Fragility," a term coined by Robin DiAngelo that explains the common inability of white people to tolerate any degree of race-based discomfort (DiAngelo 54).

Resistance to discussions of racial privilege was not the only hurdle; we also found that students viewed issues pertaining to class, gender, and to some degree, sexuality in similar ways.[7] For example, gender privilege was a topic that students frequently examined in their writing, with several students expressing views that sexism was no longer a pervasive issue and certainly not a problem in the US compared to other countries. We believe our location in Lincoln, NE and the fact that most of our students were white Midwesterners contributed to these views, particularly in regard to race, as several students in our classes expressed that the UNL campus was the most diverse place they had ever lived.[8] Navigating moments of student resistance worked best in one-on-one conference settings. Student resistance, while an expected challenge of teaching a unit such as this one, presents opportunities for learning for both students and teachers. Incorporating moments for reflection after discussions and in one-on-one settings, such as conferences, offers a space to unpack some of the resistance.

We each handled this resistance differently in our classrooms; however, we argue that feelings of guilt are a major cause of resistance to this topic, as well as one of the most common emotions students expressed during this unit when they owned their privileges. Students, especially those who are already predisposed to feel compassion or empathy for others, dislike the idea that their privilege might come at the expense of another person or group (Platt 215). As a result, students might wish to avoid discussions of these topics in order to protect their emotional states. Patience with students is key to incorporating a unit or topics surrounding privilege, as students are often thinking critically about these concepts for the first time in our courses. We must underscore the importance of anti-racist work as an ongoing practice that requires regular reflection and assessment.

The current state of the nation demonstrates the urgent need for critical conversations that engage identities, cultivate compassion, and model vulnerability in our classrooms. A unit on identity and social privilege such as we designed creates space for students to reflect on and analyze their personal experiences in a way that contextualizes them within a larger sociocultural climate. Asking students to analyze their individual experiences and social positioning moves beyond mere "confessional" writing, teaching them critical thinking and rhetorical skills that are valued in academia and in the world. As composition teachers, we are in a unique position to help students engage with these issues because we deal in representations and constructions of the self and others through writing and language. Our typically small class sizes, as well as the fact that introductory composition courses are often general education requirements, allows us to form personal connections with an array of students across disciplines. Our classrooms cultivate opportunities for students to engage often difficult discussions grounded in shared vulnerability and constructive dialogue. A unit on privilege and identity is one way that we as composition teachers can actively respond to today's cultural climate in a manner that moves beyond celebrations of diversity, instead asking students to examine what diversity really looks like in and through individuals' lived experiences. Students can use personal experience, rhetorical skills, and research to interrogate and combat stereotypes. In other words, we can work with students toward resisting single stories—whether about ourselves or people quite different from them.

Notes

1. This unit was designed and taught while Kumari and Thielen were both at the University of Nebraska–Lincoln in 2015-2016. Kumari is now an Assistant Professor at Texas A&M University–Commerce; Thielen is a PhD candidate at Case Western Reserve University.

2. Peggy McIntosh describes privilege as "a corollary of discrimination" or "the 'upside' of oppression; it is unearned advantage that corresponds to unearned disadvantage in society" (2013, xi).

3. See Case, *Deconstructing Privilege*, for a collection of pedagogical articles on privilege.

4. Additionally, these discussions of representation sought to help students avoid or complicate problematic overidentification with people whose experiences were drastically different from their own. Kathryn Johnson Gindlesparger calls attention to this problem in her examination of student study abroad writing. While we of course were not familiar with Gindlesparger's work at the time of our teaching, we share her concerns.

5. See "Framework for Success in Postsecondary Writing" (2012).

6. Heather Thomson-Bunn argues that fear of being stereotyped or eliciting instructor disapproval often results in students avoiding religion or religious discourse in their writing (380-381).

7. Because our students were in high school during the heat of the gay marriage debate, we found they are more likely to see discrimination and oppression of the LGBTQ community as an ongoing problem. Resistance to discussing sexuality was frequently tied to students' religious backgrounds.

8. Although many of our students were from Omaha, NE (and Omaha as a city is more diverse than Lincoln), most of the students we taught in these courses were from suburban areas of Omaha, which are predominantly white. These students acknowledged that they had little contact with people of other races in their everyday life.

Works Cited

Adichie, Chimamanda Ngozi. "The Danger of a Single Story." TED Talk, 18:49. Filmed in July 2009.

Anzaldùa, Gloria. "How to Tame a Wild Tongue." *Borderlands/La Frontera: The New Mestiza*. Aunt Lute Books, 1999, pp. 75–86.

Armstrong, Margalynne J., and Stephanie M. Wildman. "'Colorblindness Is the New Racism': Raising Awareness about Privilege Using Color Insight." *Deconstructing Privilege*, edited by Kim A. Case. Routledge, 2013.

Boatright-Horowitz, Su L., Marisa E. Marraccini, and Yvette Harps-Logan. "Teaching Antiracism: College Students' Emotional and Cognitive Reactions to Learning About White Privilege." *Journal of Black Studies*, vol. 43, no. 8, 2012, pp. 893–911.

Case, Kim A., ed. *Deconstructing Privilege*. Routledge, 2013.

—, and Elizabeth R. Cole. "Deconstructing Privilege When Students Resist: The Journey Back into the Community of Engaged Learners." *Deconstructing Privilege*, edited by Kim A. Case. Routledge, 2013, pp. 34–48.

DiAngelo, Robin. "White Fragility." *International Journal of Critical Pedagogy*, vol. 3, no. 3, 2011, pp. 54–70.

"Enrollment by Class Standing and Gender, Fall 2015." University of Nebraska–Lincoln, https://iea.unl.edu/dmdocuments/050_fall_2015_enrl_ class_sex.pdf. Accessed 2 April, 2016.

Ferber, Abby L., and Andrea O'Reilly Herrera. "Teaching Privilege through an Intersectional Lens." *Deconstructing Privilege*, edited by Kim A. Case. Routledge, 2013, pp. 83–101.

"Fishbowl." Facing History and Ourselves. https://www.facinghistory.org/resource-library/teaching-strategies/fishbowl. Accessed 2 April, 2016.

"Framework for Success in Postsecondary Writing." *College English*, vol. 74, no. 6, 2012, pp. 525–33.

Gindlesparger, Kathryn Johnson. "'Share Your Awesome Time with Others': Interrogating Privilege and Identification in the Study-Abroad Blog." *College English*, vol. 81, no. 1, 2018, pp. 7–26.

Grobman, Laurie. "'Engaging Race': Teaching Critical Race Inquiry and Community-Engaged Projects." *College English*, vol. 80, no. 2, 2017, pp. 105–32.

Halberstam, Judith (see also Halberstam, J. Jack). *The Queer Art of Failure*. Duke UP, 2011.

hooks, bell. *Teaching to Transgress*. Routledge, 1994.

Kynard, Carmen. V*ernacular Insurrections: Race, Black Protest, and the New Century in Composition-Literacies Studies*. State U of New York P, 2013.

Lindquist, Julie. "Class Affects, Classroom Affectations: Working through the Paradoxes of Strategic Empathy." *College English*, vol. 67, no. 2, 2004, pp. 187–209.

Masterson, Kelly. "Course Design: Expanding Perspectives of Feminism in the Composition Classroom." *Composition Studies*, vol. 44, no. 2, 2016, pp. 116–33.

McIntosh, Peggy. "Teaching About Privilege: Transforming Learned Ignorance into Usable Knowledge." *Deconstructing Privilege*, edited by Kim A. Case. Routledge, 2013, pp. xi–xvi.

Messner, Michael A. "The Privilege of Teaching About Privilege." *Sociological Perspectives*, vol. 54, no. 1, 2011, pp. 3–13.

Moss, Beverly J. "Intersections of Race and Class in the Academy." *Coming to Class: Pedagogy and the Social Class of Teachers*, edited by Alan Shepard, John McMillan, and Gary Tate. Boynton/Cook Publishers, 1998, pp. 157–69.

Platt, Lisa F. "Blazing the Trail: Teaching the Privileged about Privilege." *Deconstructing Privilege*, edited by Kim A. Case. Routledge, 2013, pp. 207–22.

Sedaris, David. "Giant Dreams, Midget Abilities." *Me Talk Pretty One Day*. Little Brown & Company, 2000, pp. 16–31.

Thomson-Bunn, Heather. "Student Perspectives on Faith in the Classroom: Religious Discourses and Rhetorical Possibilities." *Pedagogy*, vol. 17, no. 3, 2017, pp. 373–96.

Tucker, Terrance. "Teaching Race to Students Who Think the World is Free: Aging and Race as Social Change." *Pedagogy*, vol. 6, no. 1, 2006, pp. 133–40.

"Undergraduate Enrollment by College and Ethnicity, Fall 2015." University of Nebraska–Lincoln, https://iea.unl.edu/dmdocuments/050_fall_2015_enrl_ethnic.pdf. Accessed 2 April, 2016.

Waite, Stacey. *Teaching Queer: Radical Possibilities for Writing and Knowing*. U of Pittsburgh P, 2017.

Williams, Wendy R., and Kala J. Melchiori. "Class Action: Using Experiential Learning to Raise Awareness of Social Class Privilege." *Deconstructing Privilege*, edited by Kim A. Case. Routledge, 2013, pp. 169–87.

Winans, Amy E. "Local Pedagogies and Race: Interrogating White Safety in the Rural College Classroom." *College English*, vol. 67, no. 3, 2005, pp. 253–73.

—. "Cultivating Critical Emotional Literacy: Cognitive and Contemplative Approaches to Engaging Difference." *College English*, vol. 75, no. 2, 2012, pp. 150–70.

English 1900: A Writing (and Writing Program) Laboratory

Laura Hardin Marshall and Paul Lynch

Course Description

In many ways, "English 1900: Advanced Strategies of Rhetoric and Research" is a familiar first year writing course designed for the familiar curricular purpose, which White, Eliot, and Peckham have memorably named "inoculation" (17). The Saint Louis University course catalog description promises students will study "complex structures of language including its logical and persuasive possibilities" ("Spring 2019 Course Descriptions"). In the College of Arts and Sciences, where English 1900 meets the "Foundations of Discourse" requirement, the course is said to lead students "to express ideas coherently, to work with a variety of research methods, and to construct effective arguments using appropriate evidence" (Saint Louis University, "Arts and Sciences"). Despite this boilerplate, the Writing Program (WP) has striven to create a course that draws on a richer, disciplinary understanding of writing and rhetoric. The standard course structure, from which instructors are asked to fashion their own syllabi, asks students to pursue a scaffolded semester-long project. In that project, students produce the following: 1) several short, research-engaged writing assignments; 2) a major exploratory research assignment; 3) a statement of purpose that addresses (or invokes) an authentic rhetorical situation; 4) a multimodal argument that responds to that situation (accompanied by an analysis and explanation of the student's rhetorical choices); and 5) a final reflection on the student's work in the course. As they pursue these assignments, which result in 20-25 pages of writing, students continually rethink and revise their projects and the position(s) they might take. They are encouraged not just to learn but also to change their minds.

Our innovation in these assignments comes from reconceiving writing as the laboratory in which thinking occurs rather than the delivery system of the results of thinking (i.e., the familiar argumentative product). Our approach grew as a response to a complex set of expectations, including the local curricular expectations (described above), current disciplinary expectations (described later in our theoretical rationale), and departmental staffing changes (namely, the entrance of literature faculty into the writing course rotation). Because managing these expectations presented challenges for both the WP administrator (WPA) and instructors, this essay is written from the dual perspective of both: Paul (WPA) and Laura (the graduate instructor whose course is the essay's ultimate focus). Laura also will discuss how her approach to the course implemented and expanded upon the course's innovations in order to respond to 1) programmatic assessment, 2) feedback from her colleagues across the WP, and 3) her own experiences teaching two sections of English 1900 in the 2017-2018 academic year.

Institutional Context

The current iteration of English 1900 stems from three levels of institutional context: the university, the WP, and the Department of English. All three played a role in shaping the course innovations we report in this essay.

In most ways, Saint Louis University (SLU) is a typical modern university. Classified as a "high research activity" institution by Carnegie, it has 13,000 students, including 8,000 undergraduates. SLU features twelve colleges and schools, each with a distinct undergraduate core (although the university is currently working toward a universal core, set to be piloted in academic year 2021-22). English 1900 is one of the few courses that traverses those curricula, and to meet that need, the WP offers 45-50 sections of English 1900 per year, capped at 20 students.

At a Jesuit university like SLU, the fact that English 1900 is the only universally required writing course should be surprising, even shocking.[1] When the Jesuits founded their first school in Messina, Italy, in 1548, their original pedagogy was steeped in Renaissance humanism and its classical antecedents. The goal of their entire introductory curriculum—which might last several years—was expressed by the phrase "*eloquentia perfecta*," or perfect eloquence. Today, like so many schools, SLU crams what was once an entire *paideia* into a single course, which can often be satisfied by transfer or dual-credit enrollment.[2] Nevertheless, the WP had been doing its part to make sure students received significant writing practice. Until academic year 2016-17, the standard syllabus included two major research-driven writing assignments: 1) the "*dissoi logoi*" assignment, which, in familiar and traditional rhetorical fashion, required students to seek out research that contradicted the positions they were considering; 2) the "advocacy" assignment, which asked students to produce an argument directed, as much as possible, toward an authentic purpose, audience, and context. These assignments would then be followed by a major multimodal project that fit the rhetorical situation they had identified in their writing (which also included several shorter assignments). Through all this work, we were trying to create the rich rhetorical, multimodal curriculum that had been the hallmark of traditional Jesuit education.

Yet informal feedback from both instructors and students suggested that our two major research assignments—coupled with the major multimodal assignment—made for an overstuffed syllabus. Instructors felt like they had to rush some projects, and they very often found themselves jettisoning assignments that the program thought important (for example, the final reflection). In retrospect, it seems that we were essentially trying to pack two courses into one, with the effect of short-changing everything.[3] Something had to give, but what? The *dissoi logoi* encouraged seeing a problem from multiple perspectives. The advocacy assignment encouraged research, argumentation, and sensitivity to rhetorical situation. The multimodal assignment helped prepare students to write in 21st century contexts. The numerous smaller assignments facilitated revision and reflection. Everything seemed important.

Before the WPA could address these concerns, the WP faced a significant material change. Traditionally, most sections of English 1900 had been taught by graduate instructors or adjunct faculty. However, raised course caps in our two required literature courses in academic year 2016-17 meant that tenured literature faculty would begin taking a section of English 1900 as part of their regular teaching schedule.

At this point, Paul, as WPA, was faced with a potentially complicated situation. Given the literature faculty's extensive teaching experience, it would have seemed presumptuous simply to direct them to follow the standard syllabus. However, few had much experience teaching first year writing. This moment therefore seemed like a *kairotic* opportunity to invite literature faculty—in the spirit of Sonja Foss and Cindy Griffin (1995)—into a conversation about current best practices in writing instruction. Contrary to what might be expected, nine of the department's twenty-five faculty immediately volunteered to join an ad hoc committee to consider revisions to the syllabus and to teach a section of 1900. The committee spent a semester examining the curriculum, enjoying a rare opportunity to talk about "what it is that we as professors do for at least half of our living: teach" (Kameen 176). The rich discussion that emerged allowed Paul and the department's other rhetoric and composition specialists to discuss best practices and identify places where faculty were already engaging in them in their literature courses. Our 2019 Council of Writing Program Administrators (CWPA) external review from Chris Anson and Deborah Holdstein endorsed this approach, observing that "we rarely see this extent of cooperation and support for writing in most traditional English departments" (2).

Most importantly, the ad hoc committee recommended a consequential revision to the sequence of assignments: cut the advocacy assignment and make the *dissoi logoi* the course's major research project. The hope was that an expanded *dissoi logoi* would not only free up time and space for more writing and thought but also allow us the opportunity to move the assignment away from a basic (and sometimes crude) "both sides" structure. The new version would encourage student writing to be far more tentative, exploratory, and messy. In the following section, we make a theoretical case for our embrace of a more hesitant rhetoric. In the "Critical Reflection," Laura reports on how this hesitant rhetoric allowed more time for research, exploration, and creativity.

Theoretical Rationale

Jettisoning the advocacy project allowed us to look more critically and with renewed interest at the practice of *dissoi logoi*, particularly where we could take it from its historical roots. Since the beginnings of rhetorical training in the west, arguing on "both sides" of the case has ancient precedent ("*Dissoi Logoi*" in Bizzell and Herzberg 47-55; Mendelson 1-72), Renaissance antecedents (Sloane 80-130), and contemporary endorsement (Elbow 147-191; Krause). Yet we wanted to do more than simply follow what Patricia Bizzell called "the already familiar recommendation to ask students to read several essays that take opposing views on a controversial issue and then to develop their own argumentative positions" (159). Early versions of the assignment often produced nothing more than a point-counterpoint pairing of 5-paragraph essays, in which anemic counterarguments would reveal students' inability to genuinely engage contrasting opinions. In our revision of the assignment, therefore, we hoped to address three issues: 1) the persistence of simplistic habits of argument, 2) a related aversion to argument or any social engagement that might proceed agonistically, and 3) ineffective research habits, marked by the superficial hunt for the golden quotable.

We turned to the disciplinary literature in order to think through these problems. In *A New Writing Classroom*, for example, Patrick Sullivan observes that, whatever advances we may have made in our theories of argumentation, "simplistic argumentative writing is alive and well in writing classrooms in the United States" (17). Citing a number of studies on the traditional argument, Sullivan argues that "much commonly-assigned argumentative writing traps students in lower order cognitive orientations and serves to support routine, automatic, and largely unexamined ways of looking at the world and engaging complex problems" (1). Sullivan is hardly the first scholar in rhetoric and composition to observe this problem (Bizzell; Corder; Elbow; Foss and Griffin; Haynes; Jarratt; Lynch, George, and Cooper; Muckelbauer). Yet Sullivan's research (1-23), along with that of Robert Yagelski (9-38), is a good reminder that carelessness in teaching argument can encourage reactive habits of mind. In *Writing as a Way of Being,* Yagelski lays these "routine, automatic, unexamined" practices at the feet of what he calls a "Cartesian ontology." This ontology encourages an unhealthy dualism between subject and object, a split that undermines the idea that "meaning-making and truth-seeking are not only social but necessarily collaborative," along with any "acknowledgement that others' interests are as valid as his or her own" (95). Indeed, this unhealthy dualism was a feature of our first attempt at *dissoi logoi,* which asked students to argue one side of a case and then another.

Following the recommendations of the department ad hoc committee to make the *dissoi logoi* the focus of the course, Paul redesigned the assignment to encourage students to look at *logoi* without the obligation to argue them. In this, we were following what Michael Gagarin has described as sophistic practice, which was interested less in traditional argument and more in inventing novel possibilities (285). The department's revised and more exploratory *dissoi logoi* assignment was designed to encourage students to move away from "managing" their projects around preconceived conclusions and instead to dwell more on the contexts and the people involved in those arguments. This change paved the way for the innovations that Laura discusses in the final "Critical Reflection" section of this essay.

The other great problem of dualistic argumentation is that it also invites ineffective research. In their study of citation practices, Rebecca Moore Howard and Sandra Jamieson find alarming trends: 46% of cited material came from just the first page of the source, 77% of cited material came from within only the first three pages, 56% of cited sources were used just once, and 76% of cited sources were used only twice (234)—findings which do not take into consideration all of the material used by students without citation at all. These statistics indicate that students are likely not fully or genuinely engaging in the research they conduct. Instead, they start "the research process with a thesis statement", with the claim and defenses already formulated (Howard and Jamieson 231). Not surprisingly, when students do research only to support said claim, they "frequently simplify or partially misrepresent the source to make it fit their arguments" (Howard and Jamieson 234). Our pedagogical questions focused on how we might counter these habits. (The WP had already begun to do this by arranging the courses around themes—such as "Gender and Identity" and "Faith and Doubt" —which would deliberately present students opportunities to immerse themselves in a particular subject.)

But still, the problem remained: how to construct an assignment that went beyond the "already familiar recommendation" of examining opposing sides? How, in other words, could we move toward what John Muckelbauer has called a "generative rhetoric" (as opposed to managerial rhetoric), in which the work of rhetoric is not somehow prior and therefore supplemental to a proposition, but rather becomes the means by which and the context in which any proposition is articulated (20-21)? The answer seemed to lie in doing the first part of what Bizzell describes (i.e., asking students to read several essays on an issue) but refraining from the second part (i.e., asking students to develop their own positions, at least not in prose writing). The *dissoi logoi* would become an assignment reserved entirely for invention, and we would delay more conscious focus on purpose, audience, and context until the multimodal project.

In making this change, we hoped to make prose writing what Bruno Latour has called "the functional equivalent of a laboratory. It's a place for trials, experiments, and simulations" (149). By engaging in *dissoi logoi* without any irritable reaching after claim or thesis, we make writing both the means and medium for knowledge, which "is always *common* but also always *provisional*" (Cooper 185). In effect, we are not asking students to make arguments but to construct the laboratory in which arguments will be made. We take the defamiliarization even further by asking students to engage in writing, as Latour puts it, as a "means *to learn how to become sensitive* to the contrary requirements, to the exigencies, to the pressures of conflicting agencies where none of them is really in command" (qtd. in Cooper 191). Ultimately, our desire was to lead students away from preemptive certainty in order to invite a more generative rhetoric.

Critical Reflection

With these institutional and disciplinary contexts shaping our first year writing curriculum, we turn now to the course in action. During academic year 2017-18, Laura taught two sections of English 1900, both themed Technology and Media. Prior to the semester's start, she attended the yearly WP orientation, where many colleagues reported that, despite programmatic changes, students were still struggling to avoid reductive two-sided argument in the *dissoi logoi*. Laura also suspected that both the *dissoi logoi* and multimodal assignments were likely to be unfamiliar to most students, perhaps uncomfortably so (as she herself was unfamiliar with these assignments prior to orientation). With these concerns in mind, Laura decided to make two significant changes in her fall semester planning. The first was to add what she called the Rhetorical Project Overview, and the second was to ask students to consider stakeholders in each assignment. Introducing stakeholders to the assignments would (Laura hoped) incline students to think about their issues less in terms of "sides" and more in terms of the people and agents (human or otherwise) working within their issues. In making these changes, Laura wanted to strategically position students to see their issues as needing something other than simplistic argumentation; they would be unable to tackle writing in this course in the ways they may have done successfully in the past.

For most of Laura's students—who were primarily freshmen and largely from STEM fields—the first challenge was to write about an issue without furthering a thesis. In fact, Laura's students not only made it abundantly clear they preferred to write the traditional argumentative research paper, they also repeatedly attempted to do so despite instructions to the contrary. In her fall section of the course, over half of Laura's students (14 out of 19) who submitted an early brainstorming assignment presented their idea in the form of a statement or claim instead of the requested question. So, rather than asking, "who has a stake in the problem of food scarcity in our city?" the students preferred to jump to claims about the causes of food scarcity (or the benefits of recycling, or the effects of technology in the classroom, etc.).

Laura's Rhetorical Project Overview was designed to help students resist this impulse to assert and to manage the uncertainty of not yet having the "right" answer. Incorporated into the syllabus, the overview briefly explained the intentions and interconnectedness of the semester's assignments. For example, the course began with preliminary research in the form of short writing assignments (such as a digital version of Ann Berthoff's dialectical notebook, or double-entry journal). That research is then used in the *dissoi logoi*, where students would engage with *but not assert* their issue. Such a claim would come later, with the multimodal project.

Most importantly, however, this overview was not simply offered to students to peruse on their own or crammed into syllabus review day. Because orientation prepared Laura for some of the common challenges English 1900 students faced, she knew that they would need more time to process what the class was asking of them. Therefore, in the second week of the semester, Laura devoted an entire class period to discussing the Rhetorical Project Overview. This session allowed students to ask fundamental questions, such "You mean you *really* don't want a thesis in the research project?" or "But all my *other* instructors told me you could never write without a thesis statement!" or "How do you even *write* without a thesis?" Eventually, with a lot of reassurance and encouragement, the students came to see that Laura's ultimate desire was that they deeply involve themselves in an issue where the most important questions were more complex than, "Am I for it or against it?" By introducing the assignments and opening the door to talking about them and their potential sticking points, Laura hoped that students would be able to focus more on the challenging work at hand and less on making sure it was delivered in 'standardized' forms.

Positioning students to tackle the semester's early assignments, specifically the *dissoi logoi*, without asserting a premature thesis provided a challenge that was both frustrating (in their opinion) yet oftentimes productive (in Laura's). In a composition class where students were expecting the standard composition essay, the *dissoi logoi* was unfamiliar in that it asked students to explore other viewpoints and write about them in ways they hadn't before. Even with the introduction of the overview, the preliminary work many of Laura's students turned in (topic proposals, early drafts) included tendencies toward asserting a specific viewpoint. Responding to student work meant reminding those students—sometimes repeatedly—not to close off their analysis preemptively, which at times meant inviting students to extra conference meetings to work through alternative ways to express their ideas.

However, by referring to the Rhetorical Project Overview and assignment prompts, students slowly began to understand what they were being asked to do, and when they arrived at the *dissoi logoi* deadline, no one submitted a set of simplistic, dual 5-paragraph essays. Even when students presented two main "sides," they worked through their arguments in ways that showed more complexity of thought. For example, one student's *dissoi logoi* began by asking questions about recycling: Was society recycling enough? Was it a waste of other resources and costs? While these questions might have stemmed from an early unspoken bias in favor of recycling, the student's *dissoi logoi* concluded with the realization that what matters most is not—as a popular meme would have it—to recycle "*all* the things"; instead, it's about recycling the *right* materials. To help students come to recognize these moments of complexity earlier in the course, Laura emphasized the overview more frequently in the following semester, at which point only 6 of 19 students framed their initial brainstorming as a claim. This suggests that the overview was having the desired effect on disrupting students' tendency toward pre-emptive claims.

Like all interventions, the Rhetorical Project Overview occasioned other challenges. Because Laura had so emphasized the scaffolded arrangement of the assignments, students sometimes struggled to see the purpose of each assignment other than as a component of the next.[4] Put another way, the process orientation of the course challenged their expectation that a writing course is about making products. To allay these concerns, Laura would later add two things to her assignments: 1) a purpose statement that provided the pedagogical rationale for each assignment and 2) a list of the course objectives the assignment was intended to meet. With the adjustments to the assignment sheets, students in the spring semester seemed better able to see how Laura envisioned the way in which staying with the process would lead to meeting the learning objectives and acquiring the appropriate rhetorical habits of mind.

These habits of mind include taking stakeholders into consideration in any rhetorical situation. So, throughout the course, Laura used various pedagogical strategies to emphasize the significance of stakeholders and to have students practice awareness of positions outside their own. This work began with course readings that offered differing perspectives on key issues, which were then the subject of class discussion. When students began considering their topics for the rhetorical projects, they were asked to complete the low-stakes assignments that were setting them up for the *dissoi logoi* (topic proposals, brainstorming, double-entry journals, etc.). But in order to make stakeholders as visible as possible, Laura assigned the Stakeholder Analysis (Appendix

A), where students were asked to describe and visualize a minimum of three stakeholders. Students were also asked to conduct an interview with at least one stakeholder. Some students spoke with friends or family members who had only minimally relevant experiences with the topic; the student exploring recycling, for instance, interviewed her Resident Assistant. Others took the initiative to reach beyond their familiar circles and approach professionals, volunteers, and entrepreneurs in the community. The student researching food scarcity spoke with an employee with a mobile grocery store (and got a tour of the bus as well!). Overall, continuous attention to stakeholders gave students the opportunity to not only read and think about what others say about those affected by their issues but also to get a firsthand account of what those stakeholders value and believe.

As a result of these changes, the first half of the semester became an extensive tour of thinking through an issue and its stakeholders before positing an opinion. The idea was to describe as richly as possible who and what was at work and at stake before even trying to consider a position or purpose. The changes Laura made at the start of the academic year clearly had the intended effect regarding stakeholders, a concept to which most of her students easily adapted. The students' papers were not always neat and tidy, but they were definitely more diversified. For example, one student took the safe but satisfactory route of examining students', teachers', and parents' views on the issue of fidget devices in the classroom. Another student, however, took a Latourian approach by examining GMOs from the perspectives of farmers, consumers, and plants, addressing not only the wellbeing of the human agents tending and eating the food but also the health and nature of nonhuman agents, illustrating a deeper understanding of agency and actors at work in the world around us. The emphasis on stakeholders proved quite successful throughout both of Laura's sections, as nearly all of her students submitted work that attempted—at the very least—to invite to the *agon* a wider range of actors, both human and nonhuman. While some students still gravitated to a simplistic view of their issue, the emphasis on multiple stakeholders and new vantage points invited them to see the issue outside of the traditional or predictable binary, and students demonstrated greater critical awareness of those involved in their issues as well as how to ask questions and seek answers about what others see and believe.

In addition to the Stakeholder Analysis, Laura also made corresponding changes to her prompt for the *dissoi logoi* to help students follow through on the work they had been doing in the beginning of the semester. Laura felt that, while the language of the program assignment sheet hinted at the possibility of multiple perspectives, it still left too much room for pro-con analysis. This became an opportunity to adjust the framework for the assignment to allow students to continue their pursuit of stakeholders and expand their agonistic imaginations. Laura revised the assignment sheet so that any references to "two" sides, perspectives, or sections were phrased explicitly as "multiple" or "various" (see Appendix B). She also developed rubrics for the *dissoi logoi* brainstorming and rough draft stages and modified the WP-designed rubric so that each phase of the project explicitly included "stakeholder" language in the assessment criteria. Ideally, by building stakeholders more directly into the course assessment, Laura could create additional opportunities for students to move away from groups of "twos" and instead allow students to describe more robustly the arguments at play.

The changes Laura made to the course resulted in clear improvements to the ways that students thought about the issues in the world around them as well as how to see those issues *in* the world around them. After the *dissoi logoi* and in preparation for the multimodal projects at the end of the course, Laura had students create advertisements for a technological innovation (selected from any of the pre-1970 items on *The Atlantic's* "The 50 Greatest Breakthroughs Since the Wheel"). In doing so, students needed to consider their innovation through the eyes (and time) of its creation, not to see it how they see and know it today. With clever ads about the safety and health benefits of anesthetic ether and refrigeration, many of Laura's students showed considerably greater thoughtfulness and awareness of context than they had with their initial *dissoi logoi* brainstorming. For example, one student used crumpled, tea-stained paper to simulate a vintage ad for pasteurization, with a line drawing of a wine bottle and half-filled glass above the caption "Sauver votre vin. Sauver votre vie." ("Save your wine. Save your life."). In the student's reflection, she describes why she wrote the ad in French and why she selected wine—not the more commonly associated milk—as the focus (because not only does it go through the process of pasteurization but it is also the most common beverage enjoyed by French men and women of all classes, according to her research, of course).

To continue facilitating students' awareness of writing as a tool for working through issues and perspectives, Laura's future sections of English 1900 will include additional opportunities for students to explicitly identify and reflect on stakeholders. For example, the double-entry journal students complete for their research will contain sections to name and summarize the various stakeholders discussed implicitly or alluded to in each source. Additionally, Laura will prompt students in the *dissoi logoi's* concluding section to reflect more actively on their initial beliefs about their issue and how those beliefs have changed as a result of their research, to encourage them to understand and accept the value of adapting to new information.

The types of changes that Laura has implemented in the course have also begun to make a difference on a programmatic level. Starting in academic year 2019-20, the WP began work on an in-house English 1900 textbook, *Eloquentia Perfecta.* The book will include a version of the Rhetorical Project Overview to serve as an introduction to the curriculum. Additionally, each assignment will be accompanied by a list of the relevant course objectives to serve as a reminder that even when assignments may not feel "finished," they are still propelling students through important processes of composition and revision. Other changes that could not yet be implemented in the textbook will still be made available to all WP instructors via Google Drive.

Toward Pedagogical Flourishing

In his recent *Provocations of Virtue,* John Duffy reminds his readers of composition's unique reach within the American academy. Offering a rough calculation based on numbers from the National Center of Education Statistics, Duffy estimates that perhaps 5 million students a year take a freshman writing course. He asks, "Who is better positioned, then, intellectually and structurally, to influence the future of public argument in the United States than teachers of college writing?" (21). That culture, as we know, is marked by a tendency to assume that the "other side" is simply not worth listening to. The English 1900 curriculum tries to respond to this assumption by asking students to engage—and linger—in the unfamiliar. Even though the individual steps and requirements within each assignment might be commonplace (doing research, citing sources, etc.), students are constantly exploring, discovering, and composing in ways that resist foreclosure and stagnation. Our purpose is of course not to endorse "both sides." Indeed, one of the effects of thorough research is the discovery that one opinion is far more persuasive than another. At those points, students—and all of us—need to be comfortable with the thought of changing our minds. Moreover, "openness," a value instantiated in the 2011 CWPA *Framework for Postsecondary Writing,* is not cultivated by simply leaving one's mind unlocked. It is cultivated by considering contrary opinions.

Writing therefore must become the laboratory in which students perform and learn from their "experiments" rather than just report on their results, unchanged from who they were before. And when students in English 1900 do decide on a stance as they are eventually required to do, they present their claims within the unfamiliar waters of composing in a new key (i.e., non-prose media). Some students take the more familiar route of addressing established audiences, such as a school board; others, however, pursue riskier projects, such as planning a GMO food party or devising a protest against abusive mining practices. These students did not rest on the habitual but simultaneously considered message and medium, always poised for "opening again to a richer invention" (Corder 29).

As we must be. In his own upper-division teaching, Paul has moved away from traditional argument in favor of papers that richly describe various positions and what might be at stake in deciding among them. This pedagogical evolution is also reflected in his colleagues' statements about their teaching. As the 2019 CWPA report suggested, "Tenure-track faculty who have taught [English 1900] were uniformly excited about their experience, *in some cases testifying that it changed the way they teach all of their courses*" (Anson and Holdstein 2; emphasis in original). The renewal of interest in the first year course also animated the department's advocacy for enriched writing instruction in the new university-wide core curriculum. The recently adopted curriculum features a four-course, 12-credit sequence of writing and communication instruction known, in true Jesuit fashion, as the *Eloquentia Perfecta* requirement. These outcomes suggest the ways in which a writing program (WPA, faculty, graduate instructors, and, crucially, our students) can contribute to a flourishing pedagogical ecology in which individual innovation, tested and confirmed by classroom experience, can change not only writing programs, but entire universities.

Notes

1. Saint Louis University's 2017 National Survey of Student Engagement (NSSE) results suggest that SLU students do less writing than their peers at similar Jesuit and private schools (Brickhouse). Though SLU's full NSSE results are not available online, a summary from the then-provost Nancy Brickhouse notes that SLU students scored 12% below similar private schools in answer to this question: "This year, have you been assigned more than 50 pages total of writing (for papers, reports, or other writing tasks)?" Granted, the NSSE relies on self-reporting. Nevertheless, the writing scores were alarming enough that Brickhouse invited Paul, in his role as WPA, to a meeting to discuss how the university might encourage more writing.

2. For more on Jesuit rhetoric in both its historical and contemporary expression, see Cinthia Gannett and John Brereton's *Traditions of Eloquence* (Fordham UP, 2016). See also *The Ratio Studiorum* (translated by Claude Pavur, S.J., Institute of Jesuit Sources, 2005).

3. This sense was confirmed by Saint Louis University's 2019 Council of Writing Program Administrators [CWPA] Consultant-Evaluator report, which recommended a second semester of writing (Anson and Holdstein 3).

4. Laura received this feedback from a Small-Group Instructional Feedback Session offered by Saint Louis University's faculty development center, the Reinert Center for Transformative Teaching and Learning.

Appendix A: Stakeholder Analysis Assignment Description

Part of being an effective rhetorician and writer is to understand the range of people (or other agents) involved in your issue: who is affected, to whom are you writing, *how* might you speak to them? For example, though my topic might deeply involve chiropractors, my actual audience (to whom I will eventually direct my point) might in reality be tattoo artists, a group with serious physical occupational hazards. In pursuit of discovering the nature of your issue and your audience, you are being asked to conduct two main forms of case analysis and outreach, discussed below, in order to discover your key stakeholders (those most affected by your issue)

Purpose Statement (or "Why Am I Doing This?"):

Knowing the key agents involved in your issue—and what is important to those agents—is an essential part of understanding rhetorical contexts and audiences. You need to know who is involved, how they're involved, and how you can connect to those stakeholders in order to compose effectively. This two-part assignment is about exploring and expanding your understanding of who/what is at stake in your issue.

STAKEHOLDER DESCRIPTIONS:

Identify at least three stakeholders in your issue. Write a brief description or summary of each one. Then, find (or draw, if you're so inclined) several pictures of each stakeholder. (You can take pictures, but make sure you're not violating someone's rights or privacy if you do.) Select pictures that you feel highlight different aspects of each stakeholder's potential position or identity.

> Note: since these pictures are not going to be used in formal academic work, I will not ask for citations, but be sure to keep notes about what you found and where. If you plan on using any of those pictures later, for the multimodal project perhaps, you should also check the usage permissions.

Once you have your pictures, expand on your descriptions by answering a series of questions about those stakeholders. Here are some examples of the types of questions you'll want to consider: what key features or characteristics match or conflict with your initial descriptions? What characteristics aren't shown? What characteristics might be potentially useful in your future assignments? Which might be obstacles (instead of useful)? In what ways and by what texts do you think the stakeholder might be affected/influenced? Overall, see *Changing Writing* page 42 for a list of questions about audience. Mark down any important discoveries, beliefs, or ideas that you think will help you address those stakeholders more effectively.

Bring your pictures and developing analysis to class in either print or digital form for class and small-group discussions on Feb. 28 and Mar. 2.

STAKEHOLDER INTERVIEW:

This component of your analysis will be submitted in early April, but here's what you need to know to plan for it. By Apr. 9, you will need to have conducted an interview with one of your major stakeholders, *ideally* the target audience for your multimodal project (though it can just be an affected stakeholder). This stakeholder must be someone outside your typical bubble—don't just interview your roommate or your mom because it's convenient. Pick someone you have to stretch a little to reach—examples and past interviews have been of community leaders, business owners/entrepreneurs, experts in a field, etc. If you're unsure of the appropriateness of your stakeholder, please ask!

This interview can be conducted in any format (in person, via video conference, phone, e-mail, chat, etc.) as long as you discuss with an actual person the needs and interests relative to that person and/or your topic. The questions you ask and the topics you discuss are up to you, but I want you to 1) pre-plan your questions (aim for about 10) and 2) direct at least some of those questions to what issues are most important to your interviewees and what texts resonate with them most—do they pay attention to bus stop signs? Billboards? Facebook ads? What information is important to them and how can it reach them? Note: you may not get to all ten questions, and that's okay; be sure you've *planned* ten questions and include them in your notes. You should also make it clear to your interviewees that they don't have to answer a question if they don't wish to, no explanation needed.

> Pro-tip: as you are developing your questions, be cautious of making assumptions about your interviewees and their beliefs. Phrase and frame your questions to allow your interviewees to speak for themselves. I also recommend marking which questions you most want to cover; if you can't get to all 10 questions, be prepared to switch gears so you at least cover the ones you marked as important.

Once the interview is conducted, convert your notes and all of your questions (even ones you didn't get to) to a format appropriate for submission to Blackboard. This will be a lead up to your Statement of Purpose assignment (coming later).

Lastly, don't procrastinate! Arranging and conducting an interview takes more time than you think it will (hence the early warning).

Course Outcomes in Progress

1. (Start to) *design* persuasive messages for specific purposes, audiences, and contexts.
2. *Analyze* messages and arguments using a sophisticated rhetorical vocabulary.
3. *Summarize, paraphrase,* and *quote* appropriate research sources accurately and fairly.

Appendix B: *Dissoi Logoi* Assignment Description

WARNING: this assignment description is long because it's attempting to articulate an unusual, unfamiliar project. This is not your traditional argumentative research paper, so bear with me.

Over the last several weeks, you've been reading, writing, and talking about technology and the topics you've chosen to explore. Through these activities, you (should) have come to identify key issues, questions, and arguments concerning technology and your issues. You're becoming involved in a conversation and have gotten practice with the basic academic moves of summarizing, capturing ideas, and citing different kinds of texts via the double-entry journal. Next, you'll be exploring how to take those elements and use them in a researched exploration of what's at stake, who's involved, and what matters in regards to your topic.

Purpose Statement (or "Why Am I Doing This?")

In your discussion (the *dissoi logoi*) you will be exercising the ability of writing as *a way of thinking through a difficult problem,* as writing isn't simply a matter of reporting ideas so that someone else can read them. Rather, writing is the means by which you formulate your own ideas and opinions—often, you only know what you really want to say once you've written it, right? By writing through a topic and its nuances, you can prepare yourselves to eventually (not now, but later) arrive at a fully informed point or thesis about it.

The *dissoi logoi* asks you to think through a question in a systematic way. Before I explain precisely what I mean by "dissoi logoi," though, I want to explain what this assignment is NOT. It is not a standard argument paper for which you formulate a thesis (e.g., abortion should be legal, vegetarianism should be mandated by government, etc.) nor is this assignment asking you to support such a thesis with three main points. In fact, you will lose points if you produce a main thesis statement or claim. The idea of this assignment is not to come to a conclusion, but to think through various possible stakeholders and arguments as rigorously as possible. The aim is to set aside our preconceptions (as much as possible) and to fully explore all avenues of the problem, to lay out the information so that you can form opinions only after you've assessed the scope of the issue, particularly the perspectives you don't naturally gravitate toward or 'believe.'

So, how do we do this? Our chosen method is the *dissoi logoi,* an ancient Greek phrase meaning basically "contrasting arguments." This process is based on the belief that rhetoric employs the ability to see an issue, question, or problem from many sides (examples from the first Greek *dissoi logoi*: it's bad for you if your shoe falls apart, but it's good for the cobbler; death is bad for the one who dies, but good for the undertaker). Students of rhetoric—not unlike yourselves—were regularly asked to think along divergent lines, which (hopefully) helps you recognize that there are different valid responses for most points—it's all just in how you see the problem. Students are asked to do this for a few reasons.

Arguing different sides makes you learn your own arguments better. If you can anticipate objections to your ideas, you might figure out ways to articulate your ideas more persuasively. Perhaps you've had an argument like this: "I want to borrow the car. I know last time I did, I didn't return it for two days. But here's why you should give me another chance . . . ." If you've had an argument like this, you've practiced a kind of *dissoi logoi.* You know what your own arguments are, but you're also imagining what other arguments might be and planning for them. The idea here is that looking at many sides makes you a better rhetor. Arguing *dissoi logoi* allows you to observe your own ideas from the perspective of others who have their own ideas about what's important and plan potential rebuttals accordingly.

Practicing *dissoi logoi* also acknowledges that there *are* different arguments or perspectives in the first place: other opinions are valid (they may be 'wrong' or misguided but still valid). In today's public climate in particular, one side often completely ignores or dismisses the other without any consideration, a habit in which *you* should not engage. People of intelligence and goodwill can (and often do) disagree on many matters, and they can all marshal evidence and claims to support their positions. Thus, we might call this a matter of "uncertainty," meaning that, however we answer the question, we cannot be absolutely right. One side or another *approaches* certainty but never fully reaches it. These matters don't allow us to go to Google and click our way to the right response. Given these conditions of uncertainty, it makes a lot of sense to think through a question from as many perspectives as possible before forming an opinion.

Finally, another reason, which seems more important than ever: thinking through multiple sides develops your moral and rhetorical imagination. It develops your ability to see an issue from another perspective, even when—especially when—it's a position with which you disagree. You become better (in general) if you can imagine, give serious consideration to, and react to/with someone who might not share the same stance as you. Be open. In doing so, you might be surprised by what you find.

Bottom line: the point of this assignment is to dwell in uncertainty, to embrace the idea that there's not a right stance or opinion or solution, to explore the nuances of an issue to become more well-informed about its many aspects and stakeholders. Welcome and live with the likelihood of diverse responses to a complex issue, all of which can be argued with vigor.

The Stages (or "What Will I Be Doing?")

Building on your initial question proposal, improve/revise a question to ask about your issue in order to become well-informed and understand the full scope of it.

Once you have a question, (re)examine any applicable class readings and research as needed to evaluate the varying stakeholders surrounding the question you've asked.

Brainstorming

Once you've thought about your question and collected research, you will conduct a brainstorming assignment. This assignment asks you to put down your current thoughts about your topic/question and to begin forming a possible structure for your analysis. The way in which you brainstorm is up to you. In your diagnostic essays, many of you mentioned outlining; others might prefer charts, diagrams, concept maps, etc. For this stage of your assignment, you do you: what is your preferred way to prepare yourself for drafting? The only requirement I have here is that your brainstorming clearly communicates your question and shows a range of stakeholders.

Drafting

After brainstorming, formulate an essay-like (minus thesis or concluding claim) examination of your question utilizing the research you've acquired and your own critical thinking and analysis of the issue. Though the *dissoi logoi* won't do the usual things in terms of thesis, its format is not entirely new:

Set up the issue: In an introduction (1-3 paragraphs), present the central question you are asking in response to the reading you've been doing. Articulate the question, explain how you came to it or what prompted it, discuss its importance, etc. Unlike the introduction of a traditional essay, this one should <u>not</u> conclude in a thesis statement. Remember, the goal is to look openly at the topic and not yet claim a stance, but the reader should be able to see clearly what question you're trying to answer.

Body: The content of the paper can be approached in a couple of different ways, but the key is to present the major stakeholders without bias (as much as that's possible, anyway); all stakeholders are treated as valid and examined with equal vigor, detail, and research. Of course, it is not required, nor would it be practical in many cases, to present every possible stance on your question. However, you <u>must</u> present at least three key stakeholders. You might write several mini-essays, one for each stakeholder, perspective, or potential action. Perhaps you want to write a single body that toggles back and forth between stakeholders. [Note: The original wording of this section, as described in the critical reflection, read, "This section can be approached in a couple of different ways. Perhaps you want to write (at least) two sections, one that takes at one side on a given question and then a second that takes some other perspective that challenges the one that you just took. Perhaps you want to write a single essay that toggles back and forth between 2 perspectives, without finally endorsing either. Perhaps neither of these will work because you feel that the simple pro-con structure is too simple for what you're trying to do."] Overall, though, remember: to earn highest marks on this assignment, I should not be able to tell which stakeholders you 'favor' or agree with, if you do favor any (ideally, you haven't formulated a full opinion, yet!). You should be able to coherently discuss the breadth of the case, with equal detail and eloquence, which includes having balanced research. Don't tip your hand toward any side/answer.

Conclusion: Finally, in a page or a couple of paragraphs, discuss what you still need to know, reflect upon, and investigate to help you finally answer the question you're asking. The idea here is to ask yourself what further research you need to do. What gaps in information did you discover as you wrote the body? What questions are still unanswered? You can also offer here a tentative answer to your question, but I'm more interested in hearing how your understanding of your topic has changed since you first started the project. Has your mind changed or opened in any ways?

Peer Evaluations

A rough draft of your *dissoi logoi* (1,000+ words) is due after the brainstorming stage. Include in-text and end citations for the ideas and sources you've used at this stage—*never leave citation until the final draft.*

Final Draft

After peer evals, you'll continue drafting and revising to reach the 2,000+ word count (as always, the citation list doesn't count). Be sure that your draft formatting, in-text citations, and end citations conform to your chosen style guide (MLA 8ᵗʰ edition Works Cited or APA 6ᵗʰ edition cover page and References).

Course Outcomes in Progress

1. *Analyze* messages and arguments using a sophisticated rhetorical vocabulary.
2. *Summarize, paraphrase,* and *quote* appropriate research sources accurately and fairly.
3. Follow conventions (formatting, citation, etc.) of the chosen style (APA or MLA).

Works Cited

Anson, Chris M., and Deborah H. Holdstein. "External Review of the Saint Louis University Writing Program" [Unpublished, internal report]. 18 Feb. 2019.

Berthoff, Ann. E. *Forming, Thinking, Writing.* 2nd ed., Boynton/Cook, 1988.

Bizzell, Patricia. "Persuasion and Argument: Coterminous?" *Pedagogy: Critical Approaches to Teaching Literature, Language, Composition, and Culture,* vol. 5, no. 2, 2005, pp. 317-23.

Brickhouse, Nancy. "NSSE Survey Results Message." *Saint Louis University,* 8 Feb. 2018, www. slu.edu/provost/provost-communications/nsse-survey-results_2-8-18.pdf.

Cooper, Marilyn M. "How Bruno Latour Teaches Writing." *Thinking with Bruno Latour in Rhetoric and Composition,* edited by Paul Lynch and Nathaniel Rivers, Southern Illinois UP, 2015, pp. 185-201.

Corder, Jim W. "Argument as Emergence, Rhetoric as Love." *Rhetoric Review,* vol. 4, no. 1, 1985, pp. 16-32.

Council of Writing Program Administrators. "Framework for Success in Postsecondary Writing (2011)." *WPACouncil.org,* 17 July 2019, wpacouncil.org/aws/CWPA/pt/sd/news_article/242845/_PARENT/layout_details/false.

"*Dissoi Logoi.*" Translated by T. M. Robinson. *The Rhetorical Tradition: Readings from Classical Times to the Present,* edited by Patricia Bizzell and Bruce Herzberg, 2nd ed., Bedford/St. Martin's, 2001, pp. 47-55.

Duffy, John. *Provocations of Virtue.* Utah State UP, 2019.

Elbow, Peter. "The Doubting Game and the Believing Game—An Analysis of the Intellectual Enterprise." *Writing Without Teachers,* Oxford UP, 1998, pp. 147-91.

Foss, Sonja K., and Cindy L. Griffin. "Beyond Persuasion: A Proposal for an Invitational Rhetoric." *Communication Monographs,* vol. 62, no. 1, 1995, pp. 2-18.

Gagarin, Michael. "Did the Sophists Aim to Persuade?" *Rhetorica: A Journal of the History of Rhetoric,* vol. 19, no. 3, 2001, pp. 275-91.

Haynes, Cynthia. *The Homesick Phone Book: Addressing Rhetorics in the Age of Perpetual Conflict.* Southern Illinois UP, 2016.

Howard, Rebecca Moore, and Sandra Jamieson. "Researched Writing." *A Guide to Composition Pedagogies,* edited by Gary Tate, Amy Rupiper Taggart, Kurt Schick, and H. Brooke Hessler, 2nd ed., Oxford UP, 2014, pp. 231-47.

Jarratt, Susan C. "Feminism and Composition: The Case for Conflict." *Contending with Words: Composition and Rhetoric in a Postmodern Age*, edited by Patricia Harkin and John Schilb, MLA, 1991, pp. 105-23.

Kameen, Paul. *Writing/Teaching: Essays toward a Rhetoric of Pedagogy*. University of Pittsburgh, 2000.

Krause, Stephen D. "On the Other Hand: The Role of Antithetical Writing in First Year Writing Courses." *Writing Spaces: Readings on Writing*, vol. 2, Parlor P, 2011, pp. 141–52, http://writingspaces.org/krause--on-the-other-hand.

Latour, Bruno. *Reassembling the Social: An Introduction to Actor-Network Theory*. Oxford UP, 2005.

Lynch, Dennis A., Diana George, and Marilyn M. Cooper. "Moments of Argument: Agonistic Inquiry and Confrontational Cooperation." *College Composition and Communication*, vol. 48, no. 1, 1997, pp. 61-85.

Mendelson, Michael. *Many Sides: A Protagorean Approach to the Theory, Practice and Pedagogy of Argument*. Kluwer Academic Publishers, 2002.

Muckelbauer, John. *The Future of Invention: Rhetoric, Postmodernism, and the Problem of Change*. State University of New York, 2008.

Saint Louis University. "2018 Profile." *Saint Louis University*, Jan. 2018, slu.edu/about/key-facts/slu-profile.pdf.

Saint Louis University. "Arts and Sciences Undergraduate Core Curriculum." *College of Arts and Sciences*, Saint Louis University, slu.edu/arts-and-sciences/student-resources/core-curriculum/index.php

Saint Louis University. "Spring 2019 Course Descriptions." *Department of English*, Saint Louis University, Fall 2018, slu.edu/arts-and-sciences/English/pdfs/engl-coursebook.pdf.

Sloane, Thomas O. *On the Contrary: The Protocol of Traditional Rhetoric*. Catholic University of America, 1997.

Sullivan, Patrick. *A New Writing Classroom: Listening, Motivation, and Habits of Mind*. Utah State UP, 2014.

White, Edward M., Norbert Eliot, and Irvin Peckham. *Very Like a Whale: The Assessment of Writing Programs*. Utah State UP, 2015.

Yagelski, Robert P. *Writing as a Way of Being*. Hampton, 2011.

English 402: Technical and Professional Writing

Vanessa Cozza

Course Description

This course design offers an innovative approach to using client-based projects (CBPs) in technical and professional writing. It shows how teachers can incorporate CBPs in hybrid or fully virtual instruction, adapt it for a quarter or semester, and tailor it to meet students' needs. The course introduces students to and develops their skills in workplace writing, including, "[in] some cases … simply learning that a client company maintains common styles and strategies for all written work" (Wojahn et al. 132). While there are standard writing assignments, such as letters, memos, progress reports, and job application materials, other writing activities assigned depend on the CBP. These projects can involve creating operation manuals, employee handbooks, event planning guides, rewriting gaming instructions, summarizing scientific reports, producing website content, and/or compiling annotated bibliographies. The CBPs' topics vary as well, ranging from distillery operations to seed funding to grant writing.

Many college educators have incorporated CBPs in their courses (Balzotti and Rawlins; Blakeslee; Kreth; Lopez and Lee), in part because a client-based approach allows "students [to] address workplace issues by interacting with real clients in an effort to provide learners with more realistic tasks and environments" (Balzotti and Rawlins 141). Professionals from nonprofit organizations, businesses, co-ops, coworking spaces, government agencies, etc. can become the students' "clients," and the clients task students with completing writing projects needed for the workplace. According to Melinda L. Kreth, CBPs "[help] students … understand and respond effectively to 'real world' clients and their organizational contexts" (52). Students are introduced to a variety of genres and content, some of which might differ from what they learned in their college courses. CBPs also expose students to how client relationships work and often provide unforeseen challenges that become opportunities for learning and strengthening students' communication skills.

The technical and professional writing course at Washington State University, Tri-Cities (WSUTC) is a required course for undergraduates with junior standing who major in business, computer science, engineering, management, education, and other related fields. The course also fulfills a requirement for English majors specializing in rhetoric and professional writing and satisfies the University Common Requirement (UCORE) of writing communication. The undergraduate catalogue describes the course as "[research] writing: defining, proposing, reporting progress; presenting a final product; other professional writing needs" (Washington State University Catalog).

Though not all sections of technical and professional writing integrate CBPs, such a course is an ideal location for CBP integration because it serves a diversity of majors, has broad course goals, and has flexible enough learning outcomes to support client work. First, CBPs foster students' different talents and abilities and provide different ways to improve communication skills, allowing students to pursue their writing interests across a range of disciplines. In addition, juniors and seniors greatly benefit because CBPs can open possible networks, give students the kind of experience that they can add to their resumes, and/or pave the way for internship opportunities or employment.

Secondly, this course has broad enough goals to support CBP integration. This course was designed around three such broad goals:

- composing in professionally appropriate modes;
- understanding professional obligations and ethical behaviors in diverse situations;
- and working individually and collaboratively.

Finally, the learning objectives for each goal are flexible, thus providing both instructor and student with an open framework for pursuing client-based work (The learning objectives are listed in the additional materials).

Institutional Context

Started in 1946 as a single campus to meet the educational needs of Hanford, WA workers tasked with producing the first nuclear reactor during World War II, Washington State University Tri-Cities (WSUTC) became "one of the six campuses of the [WSU] system" in 1989 ("About"). The campus offered graduate-level engineering programs along with the University of Washington and Oregon State University (Haynes). It continued meeting the needs of a diverse population by increasing academic programs, expanding the campus, and welcoming undergraduates in 2007. The campus has "grown to comprise 1,841 students, six academic colleges featuring more than 50 undergraduate and graduate programs, more than 90 full-time faculty and approximately 50 adjunct faculty—each semester" (Haynes). WSUTC's collaborative relationship with Pacific Northwest National Laboratory (PNNL) and the US Department of Energy (DOE) have offered "hands-on educational experiences that lead to career opportunities," and have employed "more than 800 WSU alumni … as scientists, engineers, and other professionals" ("WSU Tri-Cities Research"). PNNL and DOE's partnerships with WSUTC have proven advantageous, offering numerous internship opportunities for engineering majors. Internships for liberal arts majors were not widely publicized. The

English department's designated internship course, for instance, did not have a formal structure for English majors, and enrolled students mostly worked internally for another English faculty member or for the campus.

My early searches for local and regional employment for students through existing relationships with professionals in the Tri-Cities area, opened up both conversations across disciplines and internship opportunities for students. I also partnered with Career Services and streamlined a formal organizational structure for internship placement and completion, which helped generate student interest. Internship information resulting from this effort appeared in WSUTC's website, offering internship opportunities not only for English majors but also for majors without a designated internship course or for students who had expressed interest in technical writing. Eventually, the program added departments with designated internship courses to the list of growing opportunities for potential student-interns. In addition, I volunteered at a local coworking space, which houses multiple small businesses. My work at the space contributed to the program's success and led to building relationships with a diverse group of professionals.

This broad, local network made it possible to pilot CBPs in the technical and professional writing course. Because internships depend on availability and because students cannot always find a position whenever they desire, the CBPs offer a similar "hands-on" experience where students apply classroom knowledge to real-world problem solving.

Theoretical Rationale

Experiential and situated learning theories (Brent; Jacobs; Lave and Wenger; Kolb and Kolb; Relles; Stein) informed the course structure and writing assignments. Alice Y. Kolb and David A. Kolb describe experiential learning in very broad terms as "[operating] at all levels of human society from the individual, to the group, to organizations, and to society as a whole" ("Experiential Learning Theory as a Guide" 11). Because of this capaciousness, this theoretical framework at least confluences with internship-related work. It offers guiding principles for designing immersive learning spaces in authentic contexts. Both approaches:

- understand student learning as taking place within an immersive learning environment where they acquire knowledge through hands-on experience and social interaction.
- see knowledge application as occurring within that same real-world context.
- call for adaptability in various situations (Kolb and Kolb, "Learning Styles and Learning Spaces" 194). By connecting students with

professionals, it immerses them into workplace culture and requires that they adapt to real-world situations by managing projects, developing written documents, working in teams, and communicating with diverse audiences.

- recognize learning as a holistic process involving authentic contexts and concrete experiences. Its holistic process "[provides] conceptual bridges across life situations" (Jacobs 50).

- necessitate a unique learning space that "[extends] beyond the teacher and the classroom" (Kolb and Kolb, "Experiential Learning Theory" 48).

The physical classroom does not have to limit what instructors and students can do; instead, students' experiences and social interactions should (Kolb and Kolb 47). Kolb and Kolb describe learning spaces as "[communities] of practice" fostered, in this course, through collaborative writing assignments. The scaffolding and sequencing of assignments guide students toward completion of the CBPs. Some assignments require students to work individually to develop self-management skills and hold themselves accountable. Other assignments require students to work collaboratively, building team skills and being held accountable by group members.

As Doug Brent has found, "Situated learning suggests that highly context-dependent skills ... are best learned—perhaps can only be learned—when learners are immersed in the real context in which such skills must be performed on a daily basis" (400). As such, the different types of assignments and CBPs prompt students to apply a variety of specialized skills, including problem solving, goal setting, decision making, and leading. The development of specialized skills through high-impact practices, such as project-based and integrative learning, allow learning from experience to occur (Jacobs 50-51).

Course Structure

The course's overall structure creates a learning space that extends beyond the physical boundaries of the classroom. It situates students in a workplace environment that involves primary stakeholders, individual accountability, and team cooperation. CBPs place emphasis on stakeholders and users, urging students to constantly consider the target audience. As Patricia Wojahn et al. point out:

> With a real audience for their projects, students can learn first-hand the complexities of analyzing an audience and the audience's interests and needs. They can also learn the provisional nature of audience requests, since feedback from clients during a given project may indi-

cate evolving expectations and interests—a frustrating but common experience. (136)

CBPs make an audience-focused environment possible, and previous research clearly outlines how to structure a course to adapt a client-based approach (Balzotti and Rawlins; Blakeslee; Burnthorne et al.; Kreth). These authors share their experiences planning and executing CBPs and advise careful consideration of course goals and learning objectives. They also guide readers through the process of finding suitable projects and dynamic clients. Client involvement is paramount as it fosters social interaction among the instructor, peers, and clients. They contribute to the unique learning space and community-building in the classroom environment. As a "community of practice," the classroom becomes a "safe" space where students can make mistakes and learn from them. Students do not experience the same accountability as they would in the workplace: they do not run the risk of losing their jobs and clients do not run the risk of losing money. Even so, the space "[exposes] students to workplace writing practices as well as to the activity systems of particular workplaces" and it offers more support and flexibility than a standard workplace (Blakeslee 176; 183).

The course structure involves clients throughout the learning process and helps build student-client relationships. It includes client meetings, team planning meetings, review sessions, and presentations. During the first two weeks of the course, clients meet students and introduce their projects. To prepare for client meetings, students and the instructor discuss possible questions, such as "What are the project's deliverables?" and "Who are the users of the project or who is it intended for?" At this point, the instructor should also gain a clear sense of client projects and in order to guide students through these planning discussions. The amount of time students spend on projects depends on its size. Students can complete small projects in 1-2 weeks, medium projects in 3-6 weeks, and large projects over the entire semester (Lopez and Lee 175). Throughout the semester, students learn about standard course content, such as project management, document design, resume and cover letter writing, and professional correspondence in tandem with project-specific content (e.g. procedural writing or reporting). Product reviews occur at least a week or two prior to submission of the final product. Clients participate in product reviews, which are explained in the next section.

Writing Assignments

The following major assignments—the client assessment, work plan, and product review—prepare students for the final presentation. The assignments demand students develop core competencies necessary in project management by offering an authentic experience in a real-world context. The client assessment, submitted individually during the third week of class, is the first step toward managing the project assigned. After the client meeting, students show their understanding of the project by discussing its purpose, target audience or users, and deliverables. They also explain the project's relevance to the course goals, and they can add questions for the client or the instructor. The assessment helps ensure that all students understand the client and instructor's expectations before proceeding to the next step in the learning process.

Students submit the second major assignment, the work plan, during the fourth week of class. The work plan requires team planning and collaborative writing. It also requires students to make decisions and arrive at consensus. It takes them through a series of steps in project management. First, students agree on each group member's role and responsibilities, such as assigning a team leader, a communications person, and an editor. Second, they decide how and when the team will communicate. Students also schedule additional group meetings outside of class time. Next, they set their team goals by dividing the project's tasks and describing how and when members will accomplish each task. More importantly, each group member initials the work plan, indicating they reviewed, understood, and agreed to it.

For the third assignment, the product review, each group member writes a one-page memo. The product review differs from traditional peer review because it relies on usability testing or involves the project's target users. Ideally, the reviewers are people who will use the document and can include employees, volunteers, customers, or community members. For example, the editor of a community paper assigned students to write interview questions for a list of businesses. The editor reviewed each group's draft and provided written feedback. Students also make arrangements to observe users as they interact with the draft, and then, to interview users afterward, asking about strengths and points of confusion. For instance, one CBP had students rewrite gaming instructions for a nonprofit, and other students—acting as product review groups—played the games using the new instructions. One or two group members were charged with observing game play and taking notes on reviewers' reactions, questions, and concerns.

After product review sessions, team members compare notes and discuss problem areas. In their memos, each student summarizes the results of the usability test and explains how they will proceed with revisions. Similar to the client assessment, the memo helps the instructor ensure all students understand how to move forward with their team's project. One or two weeks before students submit the final product, they present their work to the clients and the instructor. The presentation's limited audience helps create an authentic experience. The classroom turns into a boardroom, where students choose to use the physical space to their advantage (e.g. by rearranging the desks to form a "roundtable"). Students prepare a 10- to 15-minute presentation, begin with introductions, showcase features of their work, and gather feedback from clients to make any last-minute changes. They then submit the final product on the last day of class (or of finals week).

Critical Reflection

Four significant realizations have emerged throughout several adaptations of this course design. First, the course structure fosters an immersive learning space when using different CBPs that call for certain skills. Second, the learning space reflects a workplace environment, where responsibilities, policies, and expectations change frequently. Third, the learning space is not confined to the classroom; educational infrastructure expands to public, community spaces. Fourth, working with nonprofit organizations makes learning through experience invaluable and provide opportunities for community involvement.

Immersive Learning

Instead of covering a variety of topics, such as writing technical reports or progress reports, proposals, and procedures, students focus on specific skills and genres in an immersive learning environment. A diversity of CBPs demand the course content change, including readings, lectures, and class activities, with the awareness that course goals are not jeopardized. They allow students to practice in-depth work on a set of skills rather than immediately moving from one lesson to the next. The content in one course section, for instance, focused on strategically reading, summarizing, and designing documents. A company requested a maximum 2-page fact sheet, summarizing Hanford's cleanup proposals and writing instructions on how the public can comment on and view relevant documents. The students reviewed an example proposal and fact sheet, identifying important sections and features. They also read Elizabeth Tebeaux and Sam Dragga's chapters "Designing Documents" and "Designing Illustrations" in *The Essentials of Technical Communication* to guide them through the examples and their own writing. In another course section, the content focused on writing "how-to" instructions. A distillery requested an operation manual for new employee training, a safety guide, and a production guide, and a coworking space requested an event planning guide for employees. To learn the basics of writing instructions, the students read both Tebeaux and Dragga's chapter "Instructions, Procedures, and Policies," "Creating Rhetorically Effective Instruction Manuals" in *Writing Commons* and select chapters from David McMurrey's *Online Technical Writing*. Each group also researched additional information about the document-type specific to their CBP. When students ran into problems or had questions, the group's communications person contacted the instructor or client to ask for clarification or resources. Because some of the content is specific to each group's project, immersive learning requires students taking initiatives to learn content beyond the lessons facilitated in class.

Adaptable Learning

CBPs require the instructor and students to adapt to various situations through problem-solving and decision-making (Kennedy et al. 148). Students may have difficulty adjusting to a client-based curriculum, particularly if they are "[accustomed] to more traditional assignments or pedagogical approaches" (Balzotti and Rawlins 141). CBPs do not come with assignment sheets that overview the project and detail its requirements. Thus, the instructor needs to play an advisory role while students determine how to approach the project assigned, find potential users for product reviews, and manage communication between clients and group members. As Wojahn, et al. point out, "Collaborative teams have been found to work particularly well for solving complex problems" (131). A nonprofit organization, for example, tasked one group with creating a guide on writing grant proposals. Students needed to include a template for a short, introductory letter, a Letter of Intent, and a Frequently Asked Questions page. They started by gathering content from their client and researching how to write and design the requested documents. The team also took initiative to learn about the nonprofit's history, as well as the guide's purpose, usefulness, and intended audience. Managing communications and preparing product review sessions tested students' audience awareness. When delayed communication became problematic, students realized the chaotic schedules of their clients and managed their time around client availability. Students also learned to use software that their clients used to communicate, such as the team messaging application Slack. Course evaluations showed students finding ways to adapt to their peers' busy schedules. When their schedules conflicted, teams used video conferencing to hold meetings outside of class. In addition, students contacted appropriate users for product review sessions. For one project, students collaborated with their client's employees for the "how-to" guide they created. For another project, students asked roommates, friends, and family members to participate as target users of their document which included the general public. Adaptable learning necessitates that students become agents of their own learning, and with that, they learn through experience.

Educational Infrastructure

A stable educational infrastructure requires a space dedicated to learning and furnished with useful resources that help foster learning. The implementation of CBPs in the classroom modify the space and its structure, as explained in the previous section. For a client-based approach to work, infrastructure cannot just be confined to the classroom and the institution with social interaction between the instructor and peers. It needs to spread into public, community spaces. The institutional context described earlier and instructor engagement with outside professionals or volunteers in community spaces helps build bridges between the university and outside stakeholders. For instance, I needed to build a professional network to make CBPs an option in the technical and professional writing course. It first involved using the resources available and developing programs within the university (e.g. collaborating with Career Services, streamlining internship placement and completion, increasing student awareness and interest, and finding internship opportunities). The network became a major part of the course infrastructure, bringing the type of authentic, concrete experiences students gain from internships into the course. These relationships are what make the course immersive, adaptable, and a part of a real-world context.

Community Work

Nonprofit organizations add value to the learning experience and allow students to do community work. Lopez and Lee recommend instructors work with nonprofits because they "make particularly good clients … Nonprofits expose students to alternative business philosophies and marketing methods … build skills such as working with no or very small budgets, and can get students involved in a project that touches them personally" (174). One client, the editor of the community newspaper *Tumbleweird*, first asked students to draft interview questions for her to use when interviewing small, local businesses in the area. The client planned to help the city's small businesses by featuring one in each monthly publication. The project, lasting about 4-5 weeks, introduced students to the realities of running and maintaining a local publication that relies on community funding and support. The project also required students to get to know community members by researching the businesses and contacting owners. As Wojahn, et al. note, "Opportunities to work for a real client allow students to begin recognizing the ways in which organizations are communities with their own networks, norms, language, and rituals" (132). Students learned how to create thoughtful, open-ended questions that invited informative responses from business owners or employees to help increase the public's interest. The client contributed to students' efforts by reviewing each group's draft of interview questions and offering written feedback.

The same client, also the co-founder of a gaming organization, tasked students with a second project. Her organization hosts events where families can play different types of board games provided. The client asked students to rewrite gaming instructions for multiple card games, adult board games, and children games to make the instructions accessible. She also wanted to translate the students' instructions into Spanish and Russian for multilingual families. The client provided all board games, which made it easy for students to review the traditional instructions by playing the games, and later, use other groups to review their new instructions through game play as well. Students learned how to simplify complex language and sentence structure for certain audiences. Students expressed their appreciation for this project when interviewed for the campus newsletter (Murray).

Challenges and Future Outlook

This course design exposes students to many different fields and introduces them to professional cultures, but there is room for improvement. A future design of this course would: 1) allow internal clients to participate; 2) provide small or medium CBPs to allow time for other course-related tasks and lessons, such as resume and cover letter writing; and 3) find recording software that grants flexibility, particularly for clients who cannot visit the classroom.

External clients are ideal because they offer a realistic internship-related experience in which students work with professionals outside of the university. However, one of the challenges of CBPs includes finding external clients and coordinating schedules, visits, and communications. Recruiting colleagues as clients, including faculty, staff, or administrators, can ease accessibility and involve students in projects relevant to their education, such as writing departmental documents or student handbooks. In a different English course, for example, a History professor assumed the client-role and asked students to create a brochure for those interested in pursuing a history degree. The professor's proximity and availability allowed immediate communications and manageable classroom visits. Internal clients also give students insight into the type of workplace writing that departmental leaders, staff, and administrators do.

Whether recruiting internal or external clients, large projects can take the entire semester to complete (Lopez and Lee 175) and with unforeseen challenges, they can limit the amount of time spent on other content or lessons. Instead, small or medium CBPs leave room for other course-related content not directly connected to the CBPs. Lopez and Lee's "Five Principles for Workable Client-Based Projects: Lessons from the Trenches" offer examples of small, medium, and large CBPs. Students can complete small projects in 1-2 weeks or medium projects in 3-6 weeks. A medium CBP worked well in one section where the client tasked students with creating annotated bibliographies for scientific reports. Such medium projects left room for one or two days of weekly class time dedicated to CBP work, and course evaluations revealed that students were grateful for that time. (For those teaching in the quarter system or 6 to 12-week summer sessions, my sense is that large projects can still work well in those contexts.)

Recording software, such as Panopto or Zoom, gives clients and instructors flexibility. For instance, instructors can record clients introducing projects, answering previously written student questions, or offering summative feedback. Instructors can assign students to watch recorded videos asynchronously, while dedicating class time to other work. Recording software also can decrease the amount of time the instructor and clients spend on giving students feedback. Moreover, recordings can also replace written feedback, potentially increasing the level of comprehension by avoiding unclear written feedback. Just as importantly, students have increased flexibility for accessing course materials, revisiting client meetings, rewatching and processing feedback, and even improving presentation skills by returning to recordings of "boardroom" meetings. Taking advantage of the software available and accessible can assist the instructor and clients when presenting information, and in turn, and can help students process information.

CBPs are valuable and make the hands-on experience afforded by internships accessible for all students, "[serving] as a bridge between the academic and workplace worlds" (Wojahn et al. 132). This pedagogical approach recognizes that learning does not only occur in the classroom but also outside of it (Sahlberg 339). Drawing from experiential and situated learning theories, this course design aims to bring the internship experience into the classroom. It shows how learning spaces can become immersive environments where authentic, concrete experiences allow students to see themselves as a part of a broader community network. Multiple elements of the course design make this possible. For one, the course structure and assignments prompt students to work on relevant and useful projects that people will use in a real-world context. In addition, the emphasis placed on audience allows students to see the value and consequences of their work. They realize, for instance, that if they write unclear instructions, the primary stakeholders and users cannot perform tasks or use the students' work. The students also learn to adapt to various situations, which is a necessary skill in the workplace. The clients, projects, and users present a different set of challenges, including the need to communicate with more than the instructor and peers and the need to prepare high-quality work for more than just the instructor to see. Finally, the learning space welcomes teachers beyond the instructor because students learn from clients. They can learn about different workplace environments and gain insight into expectations and experiences in contexts outside the classroom. Much like internships, client-based approaches provide access to additional educational resources, people, and opportunities for growth.

Works Cited

"About." *Washington State University Tri-Cities*, n.d. https://tricities.wsu.edu/about-the-university/.

Balzotti, Jonathan, and Jacob D. Rawlins. "Client-Based Pedagogy Meets Workplace Simulation: Developing Social Processes in the Arisoph Case Study." *IEEE Transactions on Professional Communication*, vol. 59, no. 2, 2016, pp. 140-152.

Blakeslee, Ann. M. "Bridging the Workplace and the Academy: Teaching Professional Genres through Classroom-Workplace Collaborations." *Technical Communication Quarterly*, vol. 10, no. 2, 2001, pp. 169-192.

Brent, Doug. "Transfer, Transformation, and Rhetorical Knowledge: Insights from Transfer Theory." *Journal of Business and Technical Communication*, vol. 25, no. 4, 2011, pp. 396-420.

Haynes, Sandra. "Celebrating 30 years officially as WSU Tri-Cities." *Washington State University Tri-Cities*, 10 May 2019, https://tricities.wsu.edu/celebrating-30-years-officially-as-wsu-tri-cities/

Jacobs, Jessica. "Client-Based Project Work as Experiential Education." *Design Management Review*, vol. 30, no. 1, 2019, pp. 46-54. https://onlinelibrary.wiley.com/journal/19487169 Accessed 7 Aug. 2020.

Kennedy, Ellen J., Leigh Lawton, and Erika Walker. "The Case for Using Live Cases: Shifting/Paradigm in Marketing Education." *Journal of Marketing Education*, vol. 23, no. 2, 2001, pp. 145-151.

Kolb, Alice Y. and David A. Kolb. "Experiential Learning Theory as a Guide for Experiential Educators in Higher Education." *ELTHE: A Journal for Engaged Educators*, vol. 1, no. 1, 2017, pp. 7-44.

—. "Experiential Learning Theory: A Dynamic, Holistic Approach to Management Learning, Education and Development." *The Sage Handbook of Management Learning, Education and Development*, 2011, pp. 42-68. ResearchGate, doi: 10.4135/9780857021038.n3. Accessed Aug. 6 2020.

—. "Learning Styles and Learning Spaces: Enhancing Experiential Learning in Higher Education." *Academy of Management Learning & Education*, vol. 4, no. 2, 2005, pp. 193-212. JSTOR, http://www.jstor.org/stable/40214287. Accessed 7 Aug. 2020.

Kreth, Melinda L. "A Small-Scale Client Project for Business Writing Students: Developing a Guide for First-Time Home Buyers." *Business Communication Quarterly*, vol. 68, no. 1, 2005, pp. 52-59. EBSCOhost, doi:10.1177/1080569904273709. Accessed 16 Dec. 2018.

Lave, Jean, and Etienne Wenger. *Situated Learning: Legitimate Peripheral Participation*. Cambridge UP, 1991.

Lopez, Tará Burnthorne, and Renée Gravois Lee. "Five Principles for Workable Client-Based Projects: Lessons from the Trenches." *Journal of Marketing Education*, vol. 27, no. 2, 2005, pp. 172-188. EBSCOhost, doi:10.1177/0273475305276840. Accessed 16 Dec. 2018.

Murray, Maegan. "Simplifying Board Game Instructions for Translation into Other Languages." *WSU Insider*, 2020, https://news.wsu.edu/2020/01/29/simplifying-board-game-instructions-translation-languages/ Accessed 25 Aug. 2020.

Relles, Stefani R. "Rethinking Postsecondary Remediation: Exploring an Experiential Learning Approach to College Writing." *The Journal of Continuing Higher Education*, 2016, pp. 172-180. ERIC, doi: 10.1080/07377363.2016.1229115. Accessed 7 Aug. 2020.

Sahlberg, Pasi. "The Role of Education in Promoting Creativity: Potential Barriers and Enabling Factors." *Measuring Creativity*, edited by Eduardo Villalba, OPOCE, 2010, pp. 337-344.

Stein, David. "Situated Learning in Adult Education." *Adult Career and Vocational Education*, 1998, pp. 1-7. ERIC. Accessed 7 Aug. 2020.

Washington State University Catalog. *Washington State University*, n.d. https://catalog.wsu.edu/Tri-Cities/Courses/ByList/ENGLISH/402

Wojahn, Patricia, Julie Dyke, Linda Ann Riley, Edward Hensel, and Stuart C. Brown. "Blurring Boundaries between Technical Communication and Engineering: Challenges of a Multidisciplinary, Client-Based Pedagogy." *Technical Communication Quarterly*, vol. 10, no. 2, 2001, pp. 129-148.

"WSU Tri-Cities Research." *Washington State University Tri-Cities*, https://tricities.wsu.edu/research/. Accessed 11 Dec. 2019.

Where We Are

It's (Not) All Bullshit

James Fredal

When Harry Frankfurt's sleeper hit *On Bullshit* came out, it helped legitimized a whole new kind of academic work on the misuse of language. Unfortunately, because Frankfurt is a philosopher and unlettered in rhetoric, he presented a skewed understanding of his topic. Frankfurt believes, as have many philosophers since Plato, that the job of language is to represent reality faithfully. Either one's words correspond to the facts as they should, or they do not. Prior to Frankfurt, one could misrepresent the facts in one of two ways: unintentionally (as error) or intentionally (as lying). His achievement was to describe this third kind of failure, bullshit, which doesn't care about the truth at all and is therefore "worse than lying." This discovery was less profound than Austin's realization that words do things, but it did give humble bullshit quite a boost.

But as rhetoricians know, he got language wrong. It isn't for representing reality, it is for social engagement. Both Isocrates and Cicero tell stories of how the first humans were worse off than animals: they had no hide, no paws, no talons, no claws, nothing to protect themselves, and they were perishing. Then they were given measured language, *logos*, and with this tool, individuals were able to understand one another, to recognize and regard each other, come together, cooperate, form bonds, frame laws, establish societies, and live in peace and security (Cicero *On Invention*§I.ii.2-3, p. 6-7; Isocrates *Antidosis* §253-255, p. 327). This is myth, not archeology, but like other sophistic narratives, it reveals a profound truth. Long before language was domesticated and taught to mime "the facts," it did things. It was, as Burke says, both social tool and symbolic act.

Frankfurt's essay illustrates how misguided is our collective focus on lying, and on not caring enough about the truth, as the cardinal sin of language. In many, perhaps most instances, the central moral and epistemic problem with a speech or an argument is not that we deliberately lie or misrepresent reality. The problem is that while seeming simply to tell the truth (or not), we misuse this social tool called language. We select some "facts" and ignore others, we put these facts in one set of terms rather than another, we use resources not available to others, we manipulate conventions of politeness and decorum to quash another's perspective, we deploy media and technology to monopolize air space. And we make things: we create loyalties and hatreds, ingroups and outgroups, heroes and monsters, pedestals and boundaries. We affirm some and shame or negate others, and we often do this to exalt "us" and to ignore or diminish "them." In these and a thousand other ways, speakers—especially elite, wealthy, privileged or powerful speakers—misuse language for their own ends, to dehumanize others and empower themselves. What's worse than lying is using symbolic action to dominate others and then selectively masking or subtly flaunting this domination (Fredal). Lots of bullshit transpires without words ever being spoken.

It isn't that lying isn't wrong or important. But speaking deceptively is only one kind of symbolic offense, only one way that language goes wrong, and it is often not the most important one. Postman provides a helpful corrective: bullshit, he says, is when someone uses language to treat other people in ways that you don't approve of. Postman relativized the idea, suggesting that everyone produces what someone will call bullshit. This is true of course, but the subjective quality of bullshit does not mean that we shouldn't press forward with rhetorically informed definitions, applications and analyses of bullshit, and especially of its culturally important sources, modes, and varieties.

But it's not just bullshit anymore. Frankfurt's essay was just one wave on a scholarly tide of attention to a range of other forms of language misuse both creative and destructive. A collective term is needed that can easily refer to all of these forms. For now, I'll use "bull" for want of anything better. The list, certainly incomplete, includes bullshit, but also hoaxes, humbug, hypocrisy, demagoguery, doublespeak, doxing, dog-whistles, eichmannism, fake news, phoniness, phishing, forging, satire, skaz, parody, parafiction, pretense, propaganda, projection, bluffing, bullying, butterfly attacks, mansplaining, misinformation, trolling, shaming, chain trading, imposture, epistemic injustice, cons, conspiracy theories, alternative facts, astroturfing, and gaslighting on top of the full spectrum of cognitive biases revealed by cognitive psychology, all thriving in the media-rich soil of chauvinism, populism, and anti-intellectual revanchism. Unfortunately, our terminology remains largely colloquial, ambiguous, and in need of analysis and pruning. Many terms overlap. What ties the list together is not that they all involve some form of deception, though most probably do, but that they all manage the permeable boundary between language and power, either to point it out or to exploit it.

As a result of the Nixon White House, the Vietnam war, the anti-war and civil rights movements, the Pentagon Papers, and the Watergate scandal, rhetorical theory shifted toward the political. Karlyn Kohrs Campbell (1972) chided Forbes Hill for ignoring the glaring deficiencies in Nixon's "Vietnamization" speech; Wander (1983) accused rhetoric of being ideological. That era today seems quaint, but it may serve as an example for our times. The Trump White House, Russian election interference, extortion in Ukraine, QAnon, COVID-19 misinformation, the Boogaloo boys and the Black Lives Matter movement might catalyse a similar shift toward rhetorical interest in all forms of bull, bestowing upon Frankfurt a halo of prescience. With apologies to Churchill, never has so much been shoveled at so many by so few.

Our era moves toward a precipice and a bridge linking bull to fascism. Four features stand out, differentiating this from prior ages:

1. There are greater volumes and varieties of media-fueled bull coming from more sources higher up the institutional, bureaucratic, and corporate ladders. We see dozens of new breeds contributing to an explosion of instances. The examples are as numerous as they are obvious: Senate leader Mitch McConnell's refusal to advance a late-term Obama Supreme Court candidate before rushing to appoint a late-term Trump candidate, Trump's claims of voter fraud while encouraging his supporters to commit voter fraud, Bill Barr's pre-emptive mischaracterization of the Mueller report, Mike Pompeo's address to the RNC against the rules of his own agency, the incitement to violence that passes for patriotism on Fox News.

2. Bull is now more brazenly produced, more thinly veiled and easily disproved. Assertions widely known or easily seen to be false or self-serving are made and repeated. Little effort is expended in hiding or managing bull so that it is consistent, plausible, or seems evidence-based. No one tries to avoid the appearance that federal agencies are acting in response to Trump's tweets or that those tweets aren't informed by Fox News. "What need we fear who knows it," says Lady MacBeth, "when none can call our power to account?"[1]

3. We see more complex interactions among different types of bull, over time, through multiple forms of social media, for layered purposes, with multiple audiences, and with compound effects. An astroturfed conspiracy theory on social media is traded up the chain to a political candidate, linked to theories of a national hoax, falsely tied to a famous progressive billionaire, given credence by a gaslighting television network and amplified by bullshit tweets, all built on top of a solid foundation of lies, and fueled by a toxic mix of anti-science contempt for all those who disagree, in order to distract from widespread corruption. Analysis can no longer proceed on the basis of individual categories of language abuse.

4. An increasingly widespread and symmetrical cynicism, similar to what is seen in conspiracy theorizing, that sees both sides of the political spectrum accusing the other of the same or comparable discursive sins. A central feature of conspiracy theorizing is its penchant for imitating the practices and methods of the groups that

they attack. Conspiracy theorists use elaborate footnotes and citations to criticize mainstream academic scholarship, they justify the need for secrecy in unmasking mysterious "insiders," and they demand total and unbending loyalty in their fight against the mindless obedience of the enemy. In their naïve adherence to a black and white moral universe, they accuse the "sheeple" of criminal naiveté. Currently, each half of the population of the U.S. considers the other half to be either duped by bull or engaged in its wholesale manufacture. Both sides can't be right.

The current political age has seen virtually every known form of bull proliferate, such that whole areas of discourse are now dominated by them. One might be forgiven for suspecting that the naively sincere word had gone extinct. We will need new rhetorical tools for its examination, tools that can do justice to its depredations and work against it.

Notes

1. Spoken by Lady Macbeth in Shakespeare's *Macbeth*, Act 5, Scene 1.

Works Cited

Austin, J. L. *How to Do Things with Words*. Harvard UP, 1975.

Burke, Kenneth. *A Rhetoric of Motives*. 1950. U of California P, 1969.

Cicero. *On Invention*. Trans. H. M. Hubbell. Harvard UP.

Frankfurt, Harry. *On Bullshit*. Princeton UP, 2005.

Fredal, James. "Rhetoric and Bullshit." *College English*, vol. 73, no. 3, 2011, pp. 243–59.

Isocrates. "Antidosis." *Isocrates*, translated by George Nolin. Harvard UP, 1982, pp. 179-365.

Kohrs-Campbell, Karlyn. "Conventional Wisdom, Traditional Form-A Rejoinder," *Quarterly Journal of Speech*, vol. 58, no. 4, 1972, pp. 451–54.

Postman, Neil. "Bullshit and the Art of Crap-Detection." Paper delivered at the National Council of Teachers of English. Nov. 28, 1969, Washington D.C. Retrieved from https://www.josieholford.com/bullshit-and-the-art-of-crap-detection/

Wander, Philip. "The Ideological Turn in Modern Criticism" *Central States Speech Journal*, vol. 34, no. 1, 1983, pp. 1-18.

An Ethics of Bullshit: The Good, the Bad, and the Ugly

Joshua Cruz

Bullshit has proven difficult to define. For instance, Frankfurt claims that bullshit is not so much about lying as it is a complete dismissal of truth or falsity. Alternatively, Ball claims that "bullshit" may "cover misrepresentation, half-truths, and outrageous lies alike" (3). Just as difficult to pin down as bullshit's definition is bullshit's ethics. Some follow Frankfurt's lead, casting bullshit as a damaging phenomenon (e.g. Eubanks and Schaffer, 382); however, others suggest that bullshitting may be productive and useful in certain situations (e.g. Perla and Carifio; Smagorinsky et al.). Given the fact that we are surrounded by "fake news" and we occupy an era that has been labelled "post-truth"(e.g. Ball; Davis; McComiskey; McIntyre; Skinnell)—an era defined by its bullshit— it may be prudent to land on a definition of bullshit and determine, once and for all, how we should orient ourselves toward this phenomenon.

To define bullshit, I argue that we need to look at its rhetorical aims rather than the nature of the phenomenon itself. If that is the case, it is prudent to ask what a bullshitter is trying to accomplish when bullshitting. The literature provides us a tentative consensus: Eubanks and Schaffer refer to bullshitters as constructing a "false ethos" (383), and Frankfurt himself suggests that bullshitters "try out various thoughts and attitudes in order to see how it feels…" (35). Perla and Carifio echo this sentiment, suggesting that we try on different personalities, often that of an expert, to grow as individuals. In these cases, bullshitting is a playing at being something that one is not. This provides an aim for bullshitters: to convey a certain kind of character that is, in some way, outside of one's commonly adopted identity. Bullshit is the material that they use to do this. This does not necessarily make bullshit ethically suspect. Instead, we need to consider why they may want to convey such a character. The rest of this paper is designed to think through the potential ethical implications of bullshit: the good, the bad, and the ugly. For the sake of simplicity, I adopt a utilitarian standpoint, considering the different degrees of harm vs. benefit that may arise from bullshitting.

The Good

Perla and Carifio suggest that as we adopt new roles in life, we must perform those roles to incorporate them into our identities. In general, when we take on a new role, we have a schema for what it looks like to be such and such a person, and that schema provides us a script for certain behaviors. We are not yet the person that we want to be; by modeling these scripts, we get there. This is perhaps why bullshit is so often associated with pretending to know more than one does about a specific topic (Pennycook et al. 552). When individuals bullshit in this way, they try to convey a self that they wish they had. In a similar vein, I believe this is often what happens when students resort to bullshitting an academic essay; the difference is that students are not pretending to have knowledge so much as they may be pretending to care about a particular subject or pretending to support a specific stance, as suggested by Smagorinsky et al. or Roberts-Miller in this volume. Say we ask a student to write an analysis on a piece of assigned literature: how can we know that the student feels one way or the other, or cares to analyze the literature at all? In some cases, I suspect, the student must pretend to care, and the essay they turn in must have the patina of caring. This kind of bullshit, I argue, is not harmful. Indeed, those who pretend to know more than they do may be self-conscious enough to educate themselves in the future on certain topics; or students may find that they do, in fact, support an argument through their attempt at bullshitting one. Through the act of bullshitting, we can push our ideas farther than we anticipated (Zavattaro) and become selves that we could only pretend at being beforehand. At worst, this bullshit does no harm.

The Bad

However, one can use a false ethos for darker purposes. Certainly, Donald Trump is a prime example of instances when bullshit can cause harm. *The Washington Post* recently reported that he has uttered over 20,000 misrepresentations of truth during his four-year term in the Whitehouse (Cilliza). But do these alleged misrepresentations constitute bullshit? Well, let's consider his handling of the COVID-19 pandemic. Consider, for instance, the fact that on March 2nd, Trump stated that we would see a vaccine "relatively soon," despite the fact that experts suggest no vaccine would be available until much later; or his statement that 99% of cases are totally harmless; or that children are "almost" immune; the list goes on. These are admittedly vague claims (what constitutes "harmless," what are the limitations on "almost"?), but the point is that Trump presents himself as a kind of medical expert when he is not. Making confident, hope-filled claims (true, false, or vague) about this virus creates the image of one who knows how to handle such a medical emergency. Such politics is, as Cramer acknowledges, about identities rather than facts (as cited in Guo). This bullshit persona positions Trump so that he seems more competent, knowledgeable, and powerful than he really is. The problem occurs when we believe and are loyal to Trump's persona to the point where he "could stand in the middle of Fifth Avenue and shoot somebody" without ramification. Allowing any one person this type of power based on a perceived character—based on bullshit—undermines democracy, legality, and decency. It further creates docility when we should be taking action against a global threat that has taken over a million lives.

The Ugly

Finally, some forms of bullshit do not hold millions of lives in the balance, but its uses are still questionable. One example of such ugly bullshit exists in Daniel Whitney, better known by his stage name, Larry the Cable Guy. Whitney conveys a convincing character for his standup: a blue collar, salt-of-the-Earth redneck. The degree to which the character Larry is "real" is where we begin to see the question of bullshit emerging. On the surface, Larry is simply a character played by an actor. However, in his book, Whitney claims that regardless of his fame, he is very much Larry, and this is why his fans relate to him so well (90). It seems that Whitney wants to convince us that he and Larry are one and the same; indeed, the book itself is written *by* Larry, not Whitney, which may simply be a marketing ploy, but I suggest it is also about presentation. We develop a sense that if Whitney were not his character Larry (or vice versa), Larry would no longer be valid in the eyes of his fans. However, Whitney, in actuality, does not have a southern accent, and refers to himself as a "linguistic chameleon"—a phrase markedly un-Larry-like (Bensinger)— who is able to jump into roles easily. And Whitney is college educated (albeit he dropped out in his junior year), a stark contrast to the anti-intellectual he typically conveys. To be fair, all actors adopt a role; the question is how much he wants us to believe that he is Larry. This is ugly bullshit because it is not harmful, but it does, at least to a degree, take advantage of some group of people; it is also ugly because it is so hard to determine the degree to which it is untrue. After all, Whitney believes that he is Larry, even if we have so many signs that suggest the contrary. Like Tuco from *The Good, the Bad, and the Ugly*, there isn't anything evil happening here, but we may not like it all the same. How might fans react to learning that he does not have a southern accent? How do they feel about the fact that he is college educated? Would they be willing to pay hundreds of dollars for his shows or shell out money for his book cognizant of the fact that Larry is, in many ways, a fabrication? Is Whitney willing to admit (to his fans, to himself) that Larry is a fabrication? Here, Whitney sells a personality that his fans enjoy, but as he cashes in on his character Larry by blurring the lines between character and reality, one must wonder to what degree Larry the Cable Guy is a bullshit persona—one that helps Whitney take advantage of the redneck fans with whom he supposedly identifies.

Where Do We Go from Here?

There is no way to know the degree to which Whitney identifies with his character Larry, although we know that Larry is an exaggeration (Bensinger). It is difficult to prove the degree to which Trump believes his own medical expertise, or even whether a student is being genuine when attempting to argue a specific point for a literary analysis. We must also consider the fact that people maintain different identities at different times, and we perform those identities based on the company we keep. Who can say with certainty whether one identity is bullshit? Still, Sunstein tells us that when we attempt to forge an identity in such a way, there is always a mark of the forgery (7). This is perhaps where research on bullshit could advance; while not all bullshit is harmful, it may be beneficial to get better at sniffing it out, especially if lives are on the line. Perhaps, for instance, theories of identity or cognition could help us understand when someone is producing a bullshit persona. Discourse analysis is especially useful for determining the ways that people attempt to construct an identity for themselves, and it may be useful as we conceptualize bullshit as a fake self. We may even look to theories of embodiment to describe when individuals truly believe that they have adopted a particular identity and when their statements are commensurate with the selves they believe that they are. As we develop these theories and methods, it will behoove us to consider what exactly individuals are trying to get away with—indeed, keeping this in mind may inform such theories and methods—and we must also consider whether or not this "getting away with" may ultimately be beneficial to those bullshitting, detrimental to recipients of the bullshit, or just shitty in general.

Works Cited

Ball, James. *Post-Truth: How Bullshit Conquered the World.* Biteback Publishing, 2018.

Bensinger, Graham. "Larry the Cable Guy: My Fake Southern Accent." Uploaded 22 Feb 2017. www.youtube.com/watch?v=GsXBvzy6qiI

Cillizza, Chris. "Here's the most incredible thing about Donald Trump's problem with facts." CNN.com. Cable News Network, 21 July 2020. www.cnn.com/2020/07/14/politics/donald-trump-fact-checker-lies-washington-post/index.html.

Cohen, G. "Deeper into Bullshit." *Bullshit and Philosophy: Guaranteed to Get Perfect Results Every Time*, edited by Gary Hardcastle and George Reisch. Open Court, 2006, pp. 117–36.

Davis, Evan. *Post-Truth: Why We Have Reached the Peak of Bullshit and What We Can Do about It.* Little, Brown and Co, 2017.

Eubanks, Phillip, and John Schaffer. "A Kind Word for Bullshit: The Problem of Academic Writing." *College Composition and Communication*, vol. 59, no. 3, 2008, pp. 372-88.

Guo, Jeff. "A New Theory for why Trump Voters are so Angry—That Actually Makes Sense." *Washington Post*. 8 November 2016. www.washingtonpost.com/news/wonk/wp/2016/11/08/a-new-theory-for-why-trump-voters-are-so-angry-that-actually-makes-sense/

McComiskey, Bruce. *Post-Truth Rhetoric and Composition*. Utah State UP, 2017.

McIntyre, Lee. *Post-Truth*. MIT UP, 2018.

Larry the Cable Guy. *Git-R-Done*. Three Rivers Press, 2005.

Pennycook, Gordon, et al. "On the Reception and Detection of Pseudo-Profound Bullshit." *Judgement and Decision Making*, vol. 10, no. 6, 2015, pp. 549–63.

Perla, Rocco, and James Carifio. "Psychological, Philosophical, and Educational Criticisms of Harry Frankfurt's Concept and Views about 'Bullshit' in Human Discourse, Discussions and Exchanges." *Interchange*, vol. 38, no. 2, 2007, pp. 119–36.

Skinnell, Ryan. *Faking the News: What Rhetoric can Teach us about Donald J. Trump*. Imprint Academic Ltd., 2018.

Smagorinsky, Peter, et al. "Bullshit in Academic Writing: A Protocol Analysis of a High School Senior's Process of Interpreting *Much Ado about Nothing*." *Research in the Teaching of English*, vol. 44, no. 4, 2010, pp. 368–405.

Sunstein, Bonnie. "Be Reflective, Be Reflexive, and Beware: Innocent Forgery and Inauthentic Assessment." *The Portfolio Standard: How Students Can Show Us What They Know and Are Able to Do,* edited by Bonnie Sunstein & Jonathan Lovell, Heinemann, 2000, pp. 3-14.

Zavattaro, S.M. "In Defense of Bullshit: Administrative Utility of the Philosophically Ephemeral." 26th Annual Public Administration Theory Network Meeting. San Francisco. May 2013. Paper Presentation.

On Bullshit and the Necessity of Balance

Bruce Bowles Jr.

Asking where we are in terms of bullshit necessitates—for me at least—a discussion of where we are in terms of public discourse. And that, in turn, raises the issue of the COVID-19 pandemic. At the outset of the pandemic, I remember telling a friend that I was rather concerned about our country's ability to handle it. When he asked me why, I replied, "You can't bullshit your way out of a pandemic!" A virus is not concerned with what you believe to be correct; it operates in a cold, calculating reality immune to the oscillations of human perspectives and beliefs. Yet, while the current situation may be dire, there are valuable lessons to be learned. A pandemic puts a strain on public discourse in intriguing ways because—while there may not be any definitive, objectively correct answers about how to handle a pandemic—there are surely better and worse solutions. Bullshit might help mitigate negative perceptions or allow people to feel safer in the short-term; nevertheless, the consequences are real regardless of what you choose to believe is true. These consequences tend to accentuate the repercussions of bullshit, making its danger quite apparent.

This is why it is vital to be able to call bullshit, to point out when rhetoric is unconcerned with reality, arguing from inconsistent epistemological rules that favor its own point of view. No matter how reassuring, such bullshit inhibits discourse from generating effective solutions. However, calling bullshit can itself become a defense mechanism, a method of maintaining a particular belief at any cost—a form of bullshit itself! (After all, we rarely call bullshit on an argument with which we agree.) Calling bullshit too often can be just as damaging as not calling it at all. There needs to be a compromise, then, between calling bullshit whenever discourse digresses from our own sensibilities and calling bullshit too sparingly.

Balance, in an epistemological sense, is crucial. Discussions of bullshit tend to succumb to either a) calling bullshit on everything that does not agree with a certain "absolute" truth or b) avoiding calling bullshit at all because—it is believed—there is no true standard by which any discourse can be judged. Yet, as Joshua Wakeham contends, "Some aspects of reality lend themselves to be known and understood more easily, others resist scrutiny altogether, and many fall somewhere in between" (18). Although Wakeham is leery of settling on these epistemic discrepancies as a final solution to bullshit, I believe they are quite valuable and offer a useful heuristic. In essence, discourse concerning certain topics may never be able to obtain any degree of certainty, while rather precise facts and knowledge can be determined in other arenas. Epistemic certainty oscillates contingent upon the nature of the discourse.

These distinctions may not always be apparent, and we need to have debates about making such distinctions. This is all part of the process. But to insist that no such distinctions can be made is problematic and threatens the health of public discourse. When dealing with the COVID-19 pandemic, arguing about whether it is more productive to invest in research on treatments or research on vaccines is fair territory. Valid arguments can be made for both sides, even if one approach may appear more conducive to success than the other. There is no definitive, concrete answer. Additionally, we need to have debates about the best ways to provide economic relief for citizens and businesses; being open to a multitude of options and discussing their merits increases the chances of finding a successful solution. However, using Andrew Wakefield's debunked research as evidence that vaccines cause autism and are unsafe—while dismissing the litany of peer-reviewed research that demonstrates no causation between vaccines and autism and shows vaccines carry minimal risk—is absolute bullshit. Furthermore, arguing that no one should take a COVID-19 vaccine when a safe one (which has passed phase III testing) is ready to be distributed is outright dangerous, especially to vulnerable populations. Our knowledge of this issue possesses a rather high level of epistemic certainty that makes it fair territory to call bullshit.

In the first two instances, productive debates can be had as long as the interlocutors are willing to agree to apply norms of discourse fairly, as long as the arguments are logically consistent, and as long as positions are represented accurately (Roberts-Miller 26). On the other hand, if someone persists in holding up Andrew Wakefield's discredited research on vaccines but deems all of the peer-reviewed research contradicting Wakefield's findings as biased, it is probably not beneficial to engage that person any longer. They are probably not interested in advancing knowledge and truth but merely in maintaining their own personal truth at any cost. Being willing to empathize with others, listen carefully, and understand their position improves public discourse immensely. Nevertheless, these practices need to be reciprocal.

People tend to engage in anti-intellectual bullshit—the employment of bullshit solely to maintain but not advance knowledge and truth—when they sense their beliefs are vulnerable and they are unsure how to defend them, when they are not entirely certain why they hold beliefs, or when they have never fully thought through the values and assumptions underlying their personal truths. This is one of the biggest critiques I have of Harry Frankfurt's definition. Bullshit is not always unconcerned with truth; rather, I would argue, it can become unconcerned with certain truths. George Reisch summarizes this phenomenon well, noting that "bullshitters conceal not some indifference to truth but instead a commitment to *other* truths and, usually, an agenda or enterprise that they take to be inspired or justified by those *other* truths" (38, emphasis original). In these instances, the preservation of certain beliefs becomes paramount and leads to bullshit; paradoxically, the facts and premises upon which these beliefs are built are of little concern or importance and can be substituted or eliminated on a whim. The rhetor demonstrates a "lack of connection to a concern with truth," but only in relation to the facts and premises underlying their argument (Frankfurt 33). The truth of their beliefs, on the other hand, is a matter of the utmost importance.

It can be easy, as rhetoricians, to assume that people hold their beliefs for good reasons, that they have spent time examining them intricately. But people tend to hold beliefs for a variety of reasons not directly linked to evidence and reason. Maybe their parents believed this way. Maybe their underlying values coincide well with certain beliefs, making those beliefs welcoming, reassuring, and easy to adopt. Maybe the beliefs are embraced on the basis of group identity. Maybe the beliefs have shielded the person from having to deal with fear, protecting them from not only feeling vulnerable in regard to their beliefs but also in regard to the safety of their loved ones and themselves. In times of anxiety and fear, this vulnerability can be further exasperated; false notions about safety and the extent of the danger faced can have reassuring qualities. In all of these instances, there is a high likelihood that the belief was formed without much critical reflection.

If we offer compassion and understanding, we are more likely—but not guaranteed—to receive them in kind. In instances where fear and vulnerability may be the source of bullshit, compassion can be a powerful weapon and help to persuade people away from bullshitting to support ill-founded but comforting views. Yet, when our interlocutors are not willing to reciprocate, continuing to engage them politely exhausts resources that are better served in persuading those who are willing to debate ethically and honestly. As Jenny Rice surmises, bullshit creates blockage, which prevents productive discourse from emerging, making disgust the most pragmatic "response that exploits blockage as fundamentally unacceptable" (471). Continuing to engage bullshit only feeds it and promotes it.

Similar to the epistemic balance that must be struck, a compassionate balance must be achieved as well. Showing no compassion to those who engage in bullshit fails to account for the myriad reasons why they may be clinging to their beliefs and ignoring particular truths; furthermore, it risks alienating someone permanently. Showing boundless compassion, though, allows bullshit to permeate public discourse and to poison discussions of the utmost importance by preying on norms of respect and civility. This may appear as a promotion of cancel culture at first glance, but it is far from it. There is a difference between denying someone a platform because they hold a controversial opinion and denying someone a platform because they hold an uninformed opinion and refuse to engage honestly. The former is intellectual cowardice; the latter is intellectual honesty. What is needed is the wisdom—and self-reflection—to know the difference.

In spite of the devastation COVID-19 has wrought, it has provided us with a moment for reflection, an opportunity to learn a valuable lesson from our failures regarding public discourse. Bullshit has consequences, even if they are not always apparent. Frankfurt himself warns of this, observing how "The contemporary proliferation of bullshit also has deeper sources, in various forms of skepticism which deny that we can have any reliable access to an objective reality, and which therefore reject the possibility of knowing how things truly are" (64). Although I tend to disagree with Frankfurt in regard to bullshit being a complete and utter disregard for all truth, I am prone to defend him in regard to his views on the necessity of discourse being connected to reality. Truth may not always be as objective and stable as Frankfurt desires it to be, and we may not have unfiltered access to reality, but reality still exists nonetheless.

When we engage in bullshit in order to maintain certain "truths," when we resort to contorting facts and logic to see what we wish, we disengage from reality. Although it can be convenient and reassuring to see reality as conforming to our own perspectives, nature has a tendency to remind us this is not the case, that reality comes calling whether we understand it or not. Interpreting the COVID-19 pandemic via statistics and narratives can be bullshitted. Measuring the success or failure of certain policies in response to the pandemic can be bullshitted. The actual health and economic consequences cannot. We can only bullshit reality for so long. And, when we choose to bullshit, the damage it does may not be visible at first but will slowly start to build. Eventually, though, reality breaks through the blockage. In the end, the debt comes due—with interest.

Works Cited

Frankfurt, Harry. *On Bullshit*. Princeton UP, 2005.

Reisch, George. "The Pragmatics of Bullshit, Intelligently Designed." *Bullshit and Philosophy: Guaranteed to Get Perfect Results Every Time*, edited by Gary Hardcastle and George Reisch, Open Court Publishing, 2006, pp. 33-48.

Rice, Jenny. "Disgusting Bullshit." *Rhetoric Society Quarterly*, vol. 45, no. 5, 2015, pp. 468-72.

Roberts-Miller, Patricia. *Rhetoric and Demagoguery*. Southern Illinois UP, 2019.

Wakeham, Joshua. "Bullshit as a Problem of Social Epistemology." *Sociological Theory*, vol. 35, no.1, 2017, pp. 15-38.

On Not Bullshitting Yourself, or Your Teaching

Patricia Roberts-Miller

I have said elsewhere that Harry Frankfurt's *On Bullshit* is, well, bullshit. That was unfair. His work doesn't actually fit his definition of bullshit because his definition is one that would never apply to a member of the in-group—to us, or people with whom we identify. It isn't just a useless way to think about what makes some form of communication damaging, but a harmful way. The way that Frankfurt suggests we think about bullshit enables the derationalizing (if not actual demonizing) of out-group members while helping us hurt our shoulder patting ourselves on the back.

For Frankfurt, the important criterion is intention. A bullshitter doesn't care about what's true or false, but only about gaining compliance from the audience—it's all about the *motives* of the speaker. There are several problems with Frankfurt's argument that I'll run through quickly before talking more about what these problems mean for teaching in a culture of demagoguery.

In the first place, there are people who are engaged in the salesman's stance that we would consider ethical, even necessary. A defense attorney is supposed to be primarily concerned about persuading the jury, not to the point of violating legal and ethical principles, but because the agonistic premise of the courtroom requires that commitment to the defendant. None of us wants to be in a situation in which we could be convicted because our attorney doesn't believe us.

Second, while an author of fiction doesn't care whether what they're saying is true or false (that there might be or have been someone somewhere with this name who performed the actions in the plot doesn't matter), they do want to persuade the reader that it *could* happen. Fiction isn't true, but it has to be truthful to be effective. Similarly, the best acting persuades the audience that it's authentic, even though it's untrue. Audiences *really* believe that actors are, if not the person portrayed, then that kind of person. It's always puzzling to me that audience members think they know the inner lives and true identities of celebrities.

And that fact of (not) knowing the inner world of others is the third, and most important, problem, partially because it's a problem we are primed to deny exists. One of the most important cognitive biases is called "the fundamental attribution error" because it is fundamental to other biases. Briefly, it is the tendency to attribute different motives to in- vs. out-group members. We reason deductively from in- or out-group membership, unconsciously (but perfectly sincerely) attributing good motives to in-group members and bad motives to out-group members. Thus, if an in-group member says something false, we say they were mistaken, they misspoke—they didn't *really* lie (what

Chaim Perelman and Lucie Olbrechts-Tyteca call "dissociation"). If we have to admit it was a lie, then we tell ourselves (and sincerely believe) that they were forced into it (attribute external causes), or they had good reasons (internal attribution of blame).

It's the opposite when it comes to out-group members. For instance, an out-group political figure who says something untrue gets the least charitable interpretation possible—they were deliberately lying as part of a villainous plot. Or they are engaged in bullshit, and don't care about the truth.

Thus, because the we are *extremely* unlikely, unless prompted, to see ourselves or in-group members we admire as engaged in actions with bad intent (which is the major criterion for bullshit), but we're equally prone to attributing bad intent to out-group members, Frankfurt's project is all about hating on the out-group. Certainly, there are times when I'm not sure a lot is to be gained by trying to imagine good motives on the part of some out-groups or out-group political figures. I'm not especially interested in trying to attribute good motives to Hitler, for example, although it is worth pointing out that he was perfectly sincere and believed himself to care a lot about the truth.

What's useful in Frankfurt's kind of project is in using criteria to determine if it's worth trying to engage someone rhetorically, but I think there are better criteria than whether we think they care if they're telling the truth or lying. Are they open to persuasion? Can they name the conditions under which they would change their mind on this point? Do their arguments work together (or do the premises of one argument contradict the premises of another)? Are they willing to define terms and use them consistently? Are they willing to cite their sources?

More important, can *we* answer those questions?

What I'm saying is that Frankfurt helps us think about what jerks *they* are, but what if we're the ones being jerks? Because it's extremely unlikely that we would see ourselves as people who don't care about the truth (and if we do see ourselves that way, then we won't care that Frankfurt is calling bullshit on us), then he doesn't help us see when we aren't worth arguing with—or, more accurately, when we aren't open to deliberation. Because maybe we're full of shit.

And that point—that perhaps we're the problem—brings me to what concerns me most about teaching practices grounded in any theory that is ultimately about us (good people with good intentions) vs. them (bad people with bad intentions). We're already in a world in which people equate partisan demagoguery and political discourse. Demagoguery says there are two sides, and they map onto us vs. them. But we don't have two sides (and I don't mean that there is the option of third party voting). I mean that there are issues like criminal justice reform, decriminalizing various drugs, immigration, civil forfeiture, and others that don't break neatly into two positions (let alone two positions that map perfectly onto Democrat vs. Republican). That people might disagree on some things, but be able to work together on some policies, is how democratic deliberation is supposed to work. A culture of demagogic partisanship means that we demonize such cross-cutting policy deliberation.

I'm not saying that we need to be nice to everyone or that we should all get along. Some people are unreasonable. But not every single person who disagrees with us is unreasonable, and we're in a world in which far too many people operate on the assumption that they are. My concern is that Frankfurt doesn't help us out of this world, and in fact could easily make it worse.

For instance, were a teacher to assign the book and then ask students to identify some pundit, writer, or political figure who was engaged in bullshit, the papers would just consist of students ranting about out-group figures. Or, worse yet, the papers would be rants about figures that students believe are out-group for the teacher. I don't think students learn anything valuable out of either activity (although they might learn to bullshit pretty well if they took the second option). What I learned from teaching about demagoguery and propaganda (which have similar problems and missteps) is that the papers are more interesting and engaging if students are required to criticize an in-group member or organization. And students are more willing to do that work if the teacher criticizes in-group members or organizations and shares sample papers that do so.

As a final point, I should clarify something on which I'm often misunderstood. I do *not* think that "both sides are just as bad" or that all political positions are equally valid. I think some are unethical to the core and logically indefensible—those topics are off the table. But that still leaves a lot of positions with which I don't agree, and yet are defensible. Not all the good arguments are on my side. If we want a world in which people handle disagreement well, we have to show that disagreement (within reason) is valued in the class. And encouraging students to perceive those who disagree as people with bad motives and no reasons doesn't help.

Book Reviews

(Inter-)Cultural Literacies: Towards Inclusive Writing Pedagogies and Practices

Bordered Writers: Latinx Identities and Literacy Practices at Hispanic-Serving Institutions, edited by Isabel Baca, Yndalecio Isaac Hinojosa, and Susan Wolff Murphy. SUNY P, 2019. 268 pp.

Writing Across Cultures, by Robert Eddy and Amanda Espinosa-Aguilar. UP of Colorado, 2017. 246 pp.

Reviewed by Christina V. Cedillo, University of Houston-Clear Lake

In March 2019, compositionists met in Pittsburgh for the annual Conference on College Composition and Communication. In his Chair's Address that year titled, "How Do We Language So People Stop Killing Each Other, or, What Do We Do about White Language Supremacy?" Asao B. Inoue addressed the "steel cage of [w]hite supremacy" that determines what happens in classrooms, connecting metaphorical bars to the metal and concrete cells that claim the lives of many BIPOC[1] (353). By upholding white supremacist values disguised as the elevation of Standard Written English (SWE) and promoting grading practices based on SWE-only bias, he argued, we contribute to white language supremacy in the teaching of writing, rhetoric, communication, even English itself. So long as we continue to accept these biases, "We ain't just internally colonized, we're internally jailed," even and perhaps especially when we aim to disrupt or subvert racist norms (353). We are teaching students that the only way to succeed or be somebody is to adopt and internalize these often-implicit disciplinary mechanisms, with "disciplinary" here referring to the academic subject, bodily regulation, and the deleterious manner in which the former results in the latter.

In the days after the Address, colleagues in the discipline made known their discontent on a variety of platforms. Some did not appreciate Inoue saying that they had been "bribed" into accepting their white privilege or had helped construct that cage of white language supremacy in which we are all

1. Here I use *BIPOC* ("Black, Indigenous, and People of Color") a term meant to express solidarity among members of diverse yet sometimes overlapping ethnoracial communities to evoke how whitestream structures harm all minoritized communities. However, it's important to note that some Indigenous and Black people prefer not to use this acronym, believing it elides the specific violences that target Black and Indigenous people.

forced to exist, some of us paying with our lives. Many of us who are BIPOC scholars were disappointed but not surprised by the negative reactions. It can be difficult to be called out if you're not used to it, and to be frank, many white peers are not. As Inoue stated in urging for a "tough compassion" for our white colleagues, "They don't have the years of anti-White language supremacy training we do" (356). In other words, they must seldom engage the many different literacies required to navigate and survive in spaces never meant for us and bodyminds[2] like ours. Yet, this knowledge is required if we are to work together to make schooling and everyday life more habitable for everyone.

As educators aware of the power of language, we can make vital interventions through our teaching and social interactions, perhaps most importantly by *listening* to our students and colleagues who know through lived experience, to stories that go unheard in favor of the "real" teaching and learning of writing. We must practice a "deep listening" that deprioritizes our own habituated expectations and allows others to speak for themselves (Inoue 363). Two books that can help attune our attention and teaching to this powerful kind of listening are *Bordered Writers: Latinx Identities and Literacy Practices at Hispanic-Serving Institutions*, an edited collection by Isabel Baca, Yndalecio Isaac Hinojosa, and Susan Wolff Murphy, and *Writing Across Cultures*, by Robert Eddy and Amanda Espinosa-Aguilar. These books approach the issue of critical listening in different ways: the former looks at the diverse lives and praxes of writers from a minoritized population, while the latter provides a framework (and lessons) for teaching students to appreciate discursive and cultural differences. Taken together, these works highlight each other's strengths while extending the conversation that each alone cannot fully encapsulate.

Bordered Writers is a rare volume for our discipline that centers the voices, practices, and experiences of Latinx educators teaching at Hispanic-Serving Institutions (HSIs). A school can apply for HSI designation if their student enrollment is at least 25% full-time Latinx (3); as an HSI, the school is eligible for a variety of government grants. However, as those of us who teach at HSIs and/or are members of the Latinx community say, there's a big difference between a Hispanic-Enrolling Institution and a Hispanic-Serving Institution. Having the numbers is not enough. Teachers and administrators determine through their actions whether Latinx faculty and students are actually served. In

---

2. By "bodymind," I refer to what Margaret Price defines as "a sociopolitically constituted and material entity that emerges through both structural (power- and violence-laden) contexts and also individual (specific) experience" (271). As used in disability studies, *bodymind* deliberately challenges the Cartesian split that stigmatizes the body, denies its impact on everyday life and critical thinking, and therefore overlooks how embodied phenomena like disability and race prove epistemological architectonics.

the Foreword, co-editor of the preceding book, *Teaching Writing with Latino/a Students*, Cristina Kirklighter, explains that the individualistic approaches driving whitestream pedagogies run counter to Latinx *familismo*, exacerbating the "Latinx academic challenges of isolationism and nonbelonging" (x). Familismo exacts a promise to one's students and classmates that access and success for some will not be bought at the expense of others (xv). In this spirit, the editors confront the violence of monolingual instruction and rigid genres by including a mix of traditional academic articles and testimonios, like Steve Alvarez's *pocho* story depicting schools as "sites of hope, fear, and pressure" (16). This choice to include testimonios matters because these narratives allows marginalized people to speak, that is, theorize and claim rhetorical space of one's own. Readers from similar backgrounds should find these stories familiar while others will find them illuminating.

The essays in Part One (Developmental English and Bridge Programs) invite readers to consider what makes a learning space culturally accessible. Lucas Corcoran and Caroline Wilkinson examine New Jersey City University's "progressive" Accelerated Learning Program to argue that its monolingualism affirms "proper grammar" as the default core of writing instruction and privileges generic forms at the expense of rhetorical contextualization. Drawing on the experiences of two students, Alicia and José, they suggest how instructors may highlight rhetorical awareness while honoring students' multilingual knowledges. Erin Doran writes about the Ascender program, which includes writing- and reading-intensive courses, concentrated mentoring, and personnel training in two key concepts, *familia* and *cariño* (family and affection). Doran analyzes interviews with two-year college developmental writing faculty across Texas to show how valuing diversity and students' backgrounds can aid in Latinx student retention. Next, Jens Lloyd focuses on the experiences of a summer transition student to find that access to learning spaces can be hampered even at an "involving college," where students are encouraged to go out and get involved (60-61). Lloyd suggests that rhetorical training can help students plot "geographies of access" and make better choices regarding curricular and cocurricular activities (64). Given my own experiences as a Latina student and now a professor at an HSI, I understand the value of teaching students to traverse these geographies since this knowledge allows students, particularly first-generation college students, to locate vital resources and sustain networks of support. However, such training must incorporate the familismo and attention to multilingualism that Doran and Corcoran and Wilkinson discuss lest this instruction re-center whitestream perspectives regarding successful navigation of academic spaces. Illustrating the importance of these factors, a testimonio by Christine Garcia describes her leaving "not often progressive" yet multilingual West Texas only to encounter white supremacist curricula in graduate school (70). Together, these essays show why creating culturally accessible learning spaces requires interrogating the social, scholastic, and personal attitudes that cohere in "the discursive, bodily, and performative ways we use and judge language" (Inoue 357).

Part Two (First Year Writing) provides critical models for making vital interventions in the teaching of writing. Using a combination of theory and testimonio, Yndalecio Isaac Hinojosa and Candace de León-Zepeda draw on their experiences as multiple-identity students, writers, teachers, and researchers to explain how bodies are shaped by geographic and rhetorical locations. They provide two pedagogical tools based in the Chicanx feminism of thinkers like Emma Pérez and Gloria Anzaldúa, *reclamation* and *reimagination*, which provide means for writers to contest historical, discursive, and bodily erasure. Yemin Sánchez, Nicole Nicholson, and Marcela Hebbard follow by advancing *familismo teaching*, a culturally relevant and responsive form of pedagogy that supports students through the introduction of class families and holistic conferences. Class families provide a consistent draw and support system intended to balance the demands of life beyond the classroom. This essay proves an effective complement to previous chapters by Doran and Lloyd, demonstrating how supportive social networks can boost success. Beatrice Mendez Newman and Romeo García add to this rhetorical toolbox by highlighting the inventive potential of borderlands translingualism. As the authors make clear, it is "*not* code switching, is *not* error, is *not* interlanguage, is *not* code meshing," nor is it symptomatic of ignorance (128). Instead, translingualism reshapes genres, styles, and epistemologies in ways precluded by monolingualism and even bilingualism. As someone born and raised on the border, I concur with the definition provided by Mendez Newman and García, recognizing through lived experience how this sociopolitical cultural location cultivates a radical communicative potential white language supremacy would deny. Notably, Heather Lang's testimonio about teaching at New Mexico State University closes this section by suggesting that we learn to "embrace the untranslatable, the unassessable, the conflicting, and the shifting" aspects of meaning-making (153). As Anzaldúa famously states in *Borderlands/La Frontera: The New Mestiza*, we are our language. Therefore, we must resist racist narratives that frame Latinx language practices as deficient.

White language supremacy creates this impression of the Other's rhetorical deficiency by assuming the seemingly neutral position of the status quo. For that reason, Kendall Leon and Aydé Enríquez-Loya deploy translation as a trope for contemplating writers' relationships to spaces and/in language. They advance a writing program model based in Huatong Sun's work on "invention as articulation," proposing ways to render classroom-community connections transparent and contestable in writing so that they may be identified, analyzed, and reconstructed purposefully (161). Laura Gonzales then explains how she created a technical writing course that highlighted translation and technology, with students producing bilingual documents that addressed specific rhetorical contexts. Gonzales wants to show how working with borderlands technical writing students reveals new ways to gauge technological and cross-cultural literacies; her research and teaching reveal that the "non-standard" experiences of Latinx students can complicate and expand on traditional notions of "accessible language and designs" while problematizing static impressions of identity, language and culture (184). Isabel Baca's concluding testimonio depicts her schooling on los dos lados, her relationships with English and Spanish, and her determination to ensure her son was bilingual to show that each of us determines our own individual relationship to language. As a result, this section of the book makes clear that linguistic objectivity proves impossible because we are always writing from "somewhere."

Lastly, due to a focus on personal embodied experience, part four (Writing Centers and Mentored Writing) may be the section that most tangibly illustrates that complex web of language, power, and identity that constrains our cultural and institutional praxes. Sadly, too many Latinx instructors will find Nancy Alvarez's opening narrative familiar. Alvarez describes being told that she is "sitting in the wrong place" while waiting for her conference panel to begin (196). She is often mistaken for a patron of the St. John's University writing center rather than recognized as a tutor, even by her own classmates. Her research aims to show that Latinxs are not anomalies in higher ed, especially as our population and presence in academia continue to grow. Yet Latinx readers may also identify with the anxieties expressed by the tutors she speaks to regarding their complicated relationships to Spanish and English. Then, Heather M. Falconer shares a case from a study of the Program for Research Initiatives in Science and Math (PRISM) at John Jay College of Criminal Justice to reveal the potential success of mentored writing in undergraduate STEM courses. Emphasizing the effects of "discourse, economics, competing demands" and other kinds of borders on students at HSIs (227), this chapter attests to the ideological and political dimensions of writing and discursive access. Finally, a testimonio by Kaylee Cruz, a first-generation Latina student and tutor, closes *Bordered Writers* on a poignant note, evoking the proverbial rock and hard place that constrain many Latinx students and scholars. We enter academia only to find that we do not fit its whitely constructed spaces and still grow increasingly unfamiliar to those we love, leaving us to wonder whether we have bought into the academy's whitestream linguistic and habitual hegemony.

Given that teaching students to write ethically on their own terms is one vital means of "cutting the steel bars" of the white language supremacy cage (Inoue 364), I now turn to *Writing Across Cultures* by Robert Eddy and

Amanda Espinosa-Aguilar, a work that asks students to identify and confront their own cultural biases. This book distills many of the same insights offered by *Bordered Writers* to provide practical pedagogical support. The authors' target audience are early career educators who must learn to teach increasingly diverse student populations without replicating Standard American English (SAE) attitudes and practices that sustain white privilege. Nevertheless, *Writing Across Cultures* can assist more advanced educators wishing to help "reinvent our country, reinvent our universities, and reinvent our discipline to end all unearned group privileges of race, gender, sexuality, and culture" (xvii-xviii). Teachers at all career stages can certainly take advantage of the assignment prompts and student samples provided.

To get students "writing across cultures," Eddy and Espinosa-Aguilar present the Eddy Model of Intercultural Experience, which acclimates students to thinking about culture so they can become "polycultural." Students can then decide whether to assimilate into or isolate themselves from the dominant culture, participate in active resistance, or work across "lines of difference" (16-17). The book outlines the model's six stages, and the process is further clarified by the ongoing detailed treatment of a writing assignment that asks students to think critically about their cultural assumptions and those sustaining the space(s) they wish to enter. The six stages include the Preliminary Stage, which involves prewriting and context-building activities; the Spectator Stage, which requires that students dialogue with their classmates to find evidence of "monocultural provincialism" in their own writing (81); the Increasing-Participation Stage, during which students come to understand writing as a collaborative activity; the Shock Stage, wherein students contend with the dissonance between their "old" and "new" writerly selves and question whether they must renounce aspects of their identities in order to succeed (134); the Adaptation Stage, when students begin to view themselves as responsible to their communities and find points of connection between different cultural spaces; and the Reentry Stage, in which students realize that writing is recursive and that they have changed as a result of their learning (194). By working through writing assignments using the Eddy model, students should find "a way into linguistic agency and independence" (202), realizing that every choice is rhetorical, political, and rife with consequences.

Consequently, readers should appreciate how central rapport and care are to the Eddy model. For instance, the authors explain that they often share stories or samples of their own writing with students to reveal the dissonances they themselves experience during attempts at effective cross-cultural communication. I find this point crucial, believing that instructors should be willing to evince some of the same vulnerability that we expect from our students; only in this way can we build communities of trust. Eddy and Espinosa-Aguilar may not use the term "familismo," but a similar spirit informs their efforts to teach students to embody "center[s] of communal responsibility" (172). Like the authors in *Bordered Writers*, they demonstrate an awareness that borders are rhetorically constructed, "distinguishing those who do and do not 'belong'" and "materializ[ing] the boundaries of belonging" (Cisneros 7). They aim to undermine those boundaries so that every student—every human being—can be a subject rather than an object of writing. To effect this change, it is important to remember that "[o]ur writing is never really about us, but about those… whose stories we carry with us away from home and bring back in transformed forms" (Moraga 5-6). Sometimes that home happens to be a classroom and our peers are the family to whom we owe a debt of "communal responsibility."

Another feature that will make this book appealing to readers is the authors' disagreement regarding translanguaging. Deeming Edited American English (EAE) the "de facto language of white power" (154), the authors' ideas complement those found in *Bordered Writers* that denounce the hegemonic violence of linguistic shaming (e.g., Hinojosa and de León-Zepeda). They refuse to equate EAE with absolute correctness or establish EAE as the only code to be embraced. However, while both believe that students have a right to choose what works best, Espinosa-Aguilar argues that code-switching permits first-generation and BIPOC students the ability to navigate new spaces, while Eddy champions code meshing as a mode of resistance. Readers can thus understand that the Eddy Model accommodates diverse approaches to teaching. I do wonder, though, if this discussion, threaded throughout the book, might not inadvertently reinforce for readers some of the binary views of language that Mendez Newman and García aim to challenge in *Bordered Writers*. Binary thinking is a hallmark of white language supremacy, marking discourses and practices as either acceptable or objectionable and barring the possibility of engaging alternatives still unclassified by the academy. It would be interesting to see how the authors and other educators reframe this debate in light of CCCC's recent call for Black Linguistic Justice, which demands that teachers stop pushing students to code-switch and instead teach students about linguistic racism. Still, Eddy and Espinosa-Aguilar's work seems quite useful for drawing students' attention to the "assumptions we make about ourselves and our relationship to the world and how those assumptions guide our actions" (38). Their model provides a valuable example for those wishing to "leave space" for classroom and cross-cultural dialogues where white language supremacy can be contested.

On that note, I want to conclude this review by returning briefly to Inoue's address, to the question of "So how do we language so people stop killing each other?" (358). The logical leap required to connect language norms to people killing each other may have seemed considerable to some of those people sitting in the room that day. Fast forward one year and the nation is experiencing mass unrest prompted by the latest epidemic of state killings of Black people and other forms of violence targeting minoritized populations. From this vantage point, those once mystified connections between language and power emerge ever more clearly against the brutal consequences of dehumanizing political discourses. To people from marginalized communities, the deployment of language as a weapon of racialized violence is nothing new, and we know it goes beyond the events presented on the evening news. White language supremacy empowers the racial/izing stereotypes that make profiling possible, transforming impoverished neighborhoods into "cash cows" for local governments and for-profit prisons (Ortiz 180). Yet, at academic institutions a similar process translates the presence of minoritized students into increased government funding, with the added "bonus" that said students are forced to accept and acculturate to dominant whitestream norms. A cage is a cage is a cage.

What *Bordered Writers: Latinx Identities and Literacy Practices at Hispanic-Serving Institutions* and *Writing Across Cultures* underscore is that the failure to engage deep listening as basic respect for others' humanity authorizes serious harm. This harm does not bear out in a theoretical way on theoretical people in theoretical locations; it takes tangible forms in our classrooms and beyond, negatively affecting our students, colleagues, and even ourselves. These books encourage all of us to do our part to promote respectful communal forms of dialogue, remaining ever aware that education can change minds and lives. Ultimately, I'm hopeful that we may yet interrupt white language supremacy's violent designs.

Houston, Texas (Traditional Karankawa and Akokisa territories)

Works Cited

Cisneros, Josue David. *The Border Crossed Us: Rhetorics of Borders, Citizenship, and Latina/o Identity*. U of Alabama P, 2014.

Inoue, Asao B. "How Do We Language So People Stop Killing Each Other, or What Do We Do about White Language Supremacy?" *College Composition and Communication*, vol. 71, no. 2, 2019, pp. 352-369.

Moraga, Cherríe. *Native Country of the Heart: A Memoir*. Farrar, Straus and Giroux, 2019.

Ortiz, Paul. *An African American and Latinx History of the United States*. Beacon P, 2018.

Price, Margaret. "The Bodymind Problem and the Possibilities of Pain." *Hypatia*, vol. 30, no. 1, 2015, pp. 268-284.

The New "Available Means": Rhetoric, Ethics, and the Teaching of Writing

Provocations of Virtue: Rhetoric, Ethics, and the Teaching of Writing, by John Duffy. Utah State UP/UP of Colorado, 2019. 176 pp.

After Plato: Rhetoric, Ethics, and the Teaching of Writing, edited by John Duffy and Lois Agnew. Utah State UP/UP of Colorado, 2020. 264 pp.

Reviewed by Jamie White-Farnham, University of Wisconsin-Superior

John Duffy has been reviving the classical concept of ethics for incorporation into the teaching of writing for the past several years for good reason: a short time ago, what we were calling "incivility" in public discourse has devolved into something worse, evident in our political leaders' and their supporters' language use (and actions) built on lies, white supremacy, dehumanization, gaslighting, and purposeful, hard-to-look-at denial of facts, evidence, and reality generally speaking. While normally, "rhetoric" is always already lambasted by pundits and political observers, at the present moment—because of the weight and horrible repercussions of our worst leaders' worst examples—almost *all* language use is up for lambasting, even the most honest and earnest persons' actual attempts to speak reasonably to resolve misunderstandings or solve problems. For me and other colleagues in our field, the last few years have been an unnerving and baffling time in which to teach writing and rhetoric.

Duffy's new book *Provocations of Virtue* and its counterpart, edited collection *After Plato,* edited by John Duffy and Lois Agnew, offer cohesive reactions to "toxic rhetoric" and potential solutions to what *After Plato* contributors, Jacqueline Jones Royster and Gesa A. Kirsch, call our present moment of "*uber* challenges" (126). Both books share the subtitle "Rhetoric, Ethics, and the Teaching of Writing," and both define and reclaim the classical concept and practice of ethics for contemporary rhetorical and writing studies in today's context of a general distrust of speakers and writers in the public sphere. Recent work by Reyman and Sparby (2020) and Colton and Holmes (2018) have also revived ethics as a central principle in understanding the toxicity in public discourse on the internet. But, *Provocations* and *After Plato* offer their updated perspectives on ethics as an additional—some say forgotten or misunderstood—classical rhetorical principle a la Quintilian: teaching good people to speak/write well in the field of writing and rhetoric in particular.

Yet, each treatment of ethics is more nuanced and contextualized for the complications of the 21st century than simply referring to what Duffy calls "the Q [Quintilian] question." In particular, chapters in Duffy and Agnew's collection think globally, and both texts acknowledge—and in one case, transforms—the knee-jerk reaction that feminists might have to terms like "virtue."

Duffy continues his work of polishing a definition of "ethics," which, for many, is synonymous with moral philosophy. His definition of ethics is built in steps, identifying the concept first as a *telos*, foundation, or "language" of the work of teaching writing" (10). He suggests such a *telos* is needed in our discipline because the field is neither cohesive nor does it have an influence on public discourse in the way that it might if its purpose was to teach students to be good people through rhetorical choices, such as selecting appropriate metaphors and anecdotes and considering others' points of view. Duffy wants to help students learn to "talk to strangers" and "repair the broken state of our public arguments" (12).

Duffy positions ethics under the umbrella term "virtues," an even harder-to-define term that refers to many good qualities people aspire to evince in their characters and lives, such as honesty, courage, justice, compassion, and many others. (I counted twenty or so characteristics identified as virtues throughout the book.) Virtues in our character "enable us to make good choices, to act and react rightly, and to live as good people" (67). Thus I offer an interpretation of Duffy's title: virtue to many is a slightly mysterious and therefore provocative topic to claim for the teaching of writing–and, as Duffy points out, plenty of his audience will be provoked by a perception of "virtue" as a sexist religious concept. Duffy's purpose is to dust off its old reputation and convince us that it is not the "virtuousness" of your great-great-grandmother that kept young women subjugated and controlled in terms of sexual roles and rules (14).

To do this, he delineates a modern virtue ethics for rhetoric by explaining three ethical traditions and their rhetorical inflections in the history of teaching writing. Deontological ethics, or an ethics of rules, boils down to a prescriptive grammar, where good writing follows the rules. A consequentialist ethics prizes outcomes and therefore categorizes good writing as that which gets good grades. And, finally, a postmodern ethics inflects the teaching of writing with its critical habit, casting a good writer as one "who can absorb and articulate the fragmented moral landscape [through the] postmodern arts of interrogation and irony" (60). This is a compelling way to argue: since writing will be inflected by *some* ethic, virtue ethics—with its emphasis on being good—is the right tool to counter today's toxic rhetoric.

To me, Duffy's robust description of toxic rhetoric itself is most insightful: he pulls together recent definitions, examples, and analyses of the problem that his sources argue has been building in the US since the Reagan era. Causes include the deregulation and conglomeration of media corporations beginning in the 1980s; deep political polarization evident as early as the 1988 Michael Dukakis campaign; the ideological shifts to the far right since 9/11; and, simply, a historical acceptance of bad-mouthing opponents publicly exemplified by the nasty names Jefferson and Adams called each other (35). Duffy identifies the features of toxic rhetoric as dishonesty, unaccountability, demonization, violence, denial, and poverty of spirit, and, most importantly, he identifies the primary terrible effect of these rhetorical tactics as not only persuasive, but constitutive. The power of toxic rhetoric is that "it invites us not only to affirm or deny a given rhetorical argument, but more, to define ourselves within the terms and tropes of the rhetoric" (41). Since this is the context of public discourse, Duffy's exhortation to teach hundreds of thousands of young people a "good" framework for discourse in our first year writing classes makes sense.

Duffy's set-up is more compelling than the practical aspects of its application to the classroom, but his suggestions for how to teach within a virtue ethics framework is logical and follows directly from his claims about the need to teach good people how to write well. He offers anecdotes of how students' arguments could have landed better if they had considered their choices from an ethical point of view, and he covers how teachers can think ethically through assignments for making arguments, using evidence, considering counterarguments, and revising. The last chapter also offers gentle help for the difficulty of conducting the type of discussions that can ensue in a polarized political context and classroom with strategies such as modeling, dissensus, and creating situations in which students would imagine all the rhetorical choices available to them—a suggestion reminiscent of the ancient practice of using the *topoi* to systematically imagine and select the best of every possible approach to an argument (125).

An important final point about teaching ethics is that it is a practice. One is not born with virtues; they can be acquired and should be practiced like a skill (66). In his conclusion, Duffy turns the "Q Question" into the "P Question," a question of possibilities for the teaching of ethics in the writing classroom. This is a turn from the somewhat magical thinking of Quintilian—that the learning of rhetoric will make one a good person—to a more realistic expectation for the teaching of writing in the university classroom: when one teaches ethics, it becomes part of a routine practice of considering the available means for learners to both reflect on what they already bring to us (their backgrounds, their consumer savvy, and their political orientations) and to consider the ramifications of the language they put into the world. Duffy looks to their futures when he says: "we teach writing so that our students will speak and write as ethical human beings committed to the discursive practices of truthfulness, tolerance, justice, discernment and others" (144).

While Duffy's monograph is focused on first year writing as a seat of possibility for change and delivery of a better rhetoric and citizenry, his and Agnew's edited collection offers more range in terms of contexts in which ethics may be productively considered for attending to what they together label as "urgent ethical challenges" of our society (11). The collection is divided into two parts: "Historical and Theoretical Perspectives," and "Disciplinary and Pedagogical Perspectives" with seven chapters in each. I will take Section Two first, as I found Section One to pack a bit more of a punch than its counterpart.

The best feature of Section Two, "Disciplinary and Pedagogical Perspectives," is its purposeful discussion of ethics in as many contexts for the teaching of writing as one can think of, including assessment, the writing center, WAC/WID, training graduate students, and prison education programs. And, when higher education curricula is the focus, there are chapters devoted to teaching argument, mindfulness as ethics, and community-engaged learning. Chapters by Michael A. Pemberton and Vicki Tolar Burton represent the whole section well since their application of ethics in their contexts—the writing center for Pemberton and WAC/WID for Tolar Burton—does not yield concrete answers, but instead offers heuristics for identifying and attending to ethical questions.

Specifically, Pemberton considers how ethics applies to the complex social, pedagogical, individual, disciplinary, and institutional factors in writing center interactions, policies, and ways of helping students. Using an example of a difficult decision a tutor faced in helping a non-native graduate student with a very long, important, and technical piece of writing in one writing center session, Pemberton applies a multi-rubric of ethics, drawn from ancient and more contemporary Western thinkers, to play the scenario out in two ways, neither of which are right or wrong, and both of which are created through a heightened concern for ethics through *casuistry*, or ethical decision-making. Pemberton claims this is an appropriate path for pursuing ethics in the writing center because it "encourage[es] tutors to be self-aware and reflective, helping them analyze and articulate their own ethics of tutoring" (176).

Similarly, Tolar Burton explores the dwelling places of ethics in disciplines, including in "humble" genres such as a lab notebooks and the institutional values they represent (e.g. academic integrity, accuracy, etc.) in terms of the discipline's inquiry practices (182); in problem-solving practices and genres with a focus on rhetorical concerns such as audience and most often, the public addressed by scientific disciplines (186); in citing courses correctly across the curriculum and its various style guides (188); and in critique of performance and artifacts (190). Tolar Burton suggests that "it falls to faculty teaching WID, encouraged and assisted by WAC/WID leaders, to make clear and explicit the ethical principles that abide in disciplinary genres and ways of writing" (192). Both of these chapters reflect Duffy's claim that ethics is a practice, and I might add, an orientation similar to what Tolar Burton reminds us creates a discipline: "a way of knowing, doing, and writing" (Carter qtd. in Tolar Burton 179).

Section One of *After Plato,* "Historical and Theoretical Perspectives," is a hard act to follow, and I was spellbound by almost every chapter, which convey imaginatively wide landscapes of what ethics are, who constructs them, and where they apply.

Chapters by Lois Agnew and James Porter offer what amounts to a mini-master course in rhetorical history. In "Reimagining the Ethics of Style," Agnew traces the role of style through two major historical periods of the rhetorical tradition to trouble the idea that style is simply the reflection of an individual's rhetorical preference. Agnew argues that style can better serve the present moment of uncivil discourse in an ethical dimension as a way to highlight difference and call on the imagination to diversify language use and hence political and social perspectives. She reviews the Phaedrus, Isocrates, and Cicero's arguments on the role of style in the rhetor's ability to use rhetoric for its important purposes of contributing to society, not as mere decoration: "The assumption that language has a fundamental role in the formation of a healthy society appears for many ancient and early modern theorists to connect naturally with the idea that both intellectual growth and social relationships are achieved through attention to style. Yet [...] various developments within and beyond the academy have altered perceptions concerning the value of style" (55). Citing Porter's chapter, Agnew attributes this alteration to Plato, Ramus, and 17th century thinkers like Locke and Sprat who believed that too many ancients imprinted their imaginations on the "truth." In the opening chapter, "Recovering a Good Rhetoric: Rhetoric as Techne and Praxis," Porter provides a stunning and succinct history of the discrediting of rhetoric and an explanation of how virtue, ethics, logic, and even the artistic parts of writing such as style were lost (taken!) from the field. I would call these two chapters required reading for any rhetorical scholars committed to standing up for our perpetual underdog.

A needed counterbalance to a focus on Western traditions, the three middle chapters by Bo Wang, Rasha Diab, and Xiaoye You bring in Confucian, transnational, and translingual notions of ethics, respectively. You, in particular, points out that foundational thinkers and writers in Eastern and Western traditions of rhetoric and ethics—namely, Confucius, Plato, Aristotle, and Diogenes—were translingual, using words from their contemporaries' languages and cultures within their own (such as the North African colonies of Greece for Aristotle, for instance). This little-explored fact prefaces You's argument that "negotiating with or breaking away from the authorized system [of language] is a common practice in everyday language use and is even more critical for those who have to cross language and cultural boundaries to survive or prosper" (104). This perspective pairs nicely with Diab's consideration of what a transnational perspective on ethics offers to the teaching of writing and rhetoric, which defines transnationalism and analyzes the reception of two viral photos of three-year-old Aylan Kurdi, a little boy who drowned while fleeing Syria with his family in 2015. Diab offers possibly the most challenging ethics of the two books for a middle-class, white American like me: "Considering the photo and transnational persons through a relational lens resists 'aestheticizing border crossing or disseminating images of dead bodies while cropping them out of sight when alive'" (97). I would characterize this as an ethics of not looking away.

In a similar spirit of looking to solve the "*uber* challenges" of our world through non-Western (or at least blended) traditions, Jacqueline Jones Royster and Gesa Kirsch bring their inspiring reach-for-the-stars practicality to a discussion of ethical feminist scholarship, new materialism, a de-centering of humans as the only action-oriented agents, and two instances of the idea of "mattering"—the explosive 2018 Watson conference keynote address and the 2018 Western States Conference on Matter and Mattering, which emphasized non-western ways of knowing (121). Royster and Kirsch suggest strategies and practices for listening and responding skills, abilities for interacting with others, and capacities for engaging in respectful and sustainable dialogues to collaboratively address these challenges and create and sustain peace.

Far different in their source of ethics and site of application, Royster and Kirsch's chapter connects the collection to Duffy's monograph through their discussions of the purpose and framing of education as a way to attend to global problems, whether material or discursive. The scholars and many contributors in *After Plato* offer contemporary reasons and ethical frameworks to answer Duffy's call: teach people to use communication to solve problems for the betterment of humanity. The comparison of these writings begs the question: which is more persuasive or workable–diving deeper into our rhetorical traditions and interpreting them for a 21st century ethical emergency, or scanning wider than the Western philosophical canon to consider perspectives such as Confucian, indigenous, feminist, mindfulness, or new materialism to do the same? I am personally drawn to a both/and claim here, which I believe reflects the ethical orientation toward argument, rhetoric, and writing that each book endorses: considering all points of view, responding appropriately for the current reality, and benefitting many over few are the new "available means" (Duffy 144).

For citizens, rhetoricians, and writing teachers who are more than tired of and beyond vexed by toxic rhetoric, I urge readers to consider these texts' claims about and for ethics as a thought-provoking addition to (or revival of) our field's arsenal of principles on which to rely in a moment when many of them—reason, evidence, academic integrity, acknowledging bias, considering multiple perspectives, etc.—are not mounting the strong defense against toxicity that we would like. Both *Provocations* and *After Plato* deepened and complicated my understandings of classical rhetoric and ethics, its ancient counterparts, and contemporary locations and frameworks for ethics as well. They gave me more reasons, energy, and hope for continuing to fight the good fight.

Superior, Wisconsin

Works Cited

Colton, Jared S., and Steve Holmes. *Rhetoric, Technology, and the Virtues*. Utah State UP, 2018.

Duffy, John. "The Good Writer: Virtue Ethics and the Teaching of Writing." *College English*, vol. 79, no. 3, 2017, pp. 229–50.

Duffy, John, et al. "Special Section: Rhetoric and Ethics." *Journal of the Assembly for Expanded Perspectives on Learning*, vol. 21, 2015–2016.

Reyman, Jessica, and Erika M. Sparby. *Digital Ethics: Rhetoric and Responsibility in Online Aggression*. Routledge, 2020.

Changing the Subject: A Theory of Rhetorical Empathy, by Lisa Blankenship. Utah State UP, 2019. 160 pp.

Reviewed by Lydia Wilkes, Idaho State University

Chasms of difference between political, ideological, and cultural groups seem only to widen with each passing year. And yet we want to connect across these differences, particularly when they separate us from loved ones. Lisa Blankenship offers rhetorical empathy as way to do this hard, necessary work in her timely monograph, *Changing the Subject: A Theory of Rhetorical Empathy.* Building on Krista Ratcliffe's rhetorical listening, Blankenship contributes an ethical, deliberative theory and praxis of rhetoric with rhetorical empathy. As applicable to the contentious holiday dinner table as the composition classroom, rhetorical empathy has the capacity to influence composition theory and practice as thoroughly as rhetorical listening has. Blankenship's argument for combining personal narratives with argumentation in writing instruction also stands to influence composition pedagogy at all levels with significant implications for civic life.

As she explains in, "Introduction: Changing the Subject," Blankenship was motivated by a desire to connect across difference as a queer white woman from a conservative Christian family who experienced rejection when, as an adult, she came out. Blankenship developed rhetorical empathy as "both a topos and a trope, a choice and habit of mind that invents and invites discourse informed by deep listening and its resulting emotion" (5). Unlike the agonistic Aristotelian rhetoric still dominant in US culture and higher education, rhetorical empathy "shift[s] the focus of rhetoric from (only) changing an audience to changing oneself (as well)" (18). Rhetorical empathy involves heeding emotion, listening to personal stories, and becoming vulnerable enough to change oneself as part of an ethical rhetorical engagement. "At its core," Blankenship writes, rhetorical empathy is "a deliberative praxis that offers ways of being-with-others" (28), even when—especially when—those others make "our blood boil" (10).

Crucially, rhetorical empathy is sensitive to privilege and power. Those of us with privilege and power who are committed to justice must embrace vulnerability and examine our biases and limited perspectives. This work is not optional. For people who do not have much power or privilege, rhetorical empathy "can help [...] sustain efforts to fight the status quo and to maintain perspective [...] in the midst of polarization and, in some cases, deep and traumatic injustice" (11). Rhetorical empathy's flexible applicability ensures that people can use it strategically, if they choose to, depending on their relative status in any discursive exchange.

Blankenship develops the concept of rhetorical empathy in chapter one, "A Brief History of Empathy," with ten paths of thought about empathy in Western and non-Western traditions. Though the chapter is lengthy and wide-ranging, Blankenship's deft writing articulates complex, intersecting ideas such that Chinese *bian* and Arab-Islamic *sulh* mutually inform Aristotelian pity and the parable of the Good Samaritan. After reviewing challenges to Aristotle's rhetoric-as-persuasion by Kenneth Burke and Carl Rogers, Blankenship traces empathy in recent rhetorical theories and feminist rhetorical praxis to show how these elements overlap with thirty years of scholarship by feminist rhetorical theorists-practitioners. This tapestry of intersecting ideas illustrates rhetorical empathy's conceptual richness and cross-cultural resonances and provides each reader with paths they might explore further.

In chapter two, "Threads of Feminist Rhetorical Practices: Storytelling and Empathy from Gilded Age Chicago to Facebook," Blankenship analyzes rhetorical empathy in Jane Addams's 19th century speeches in the US and Joyce Fernandes' 21st century Facebook posts in Brazil, both of which advocate for the rights of women of color who perform domestic work. Both Addams and Fernandes use rhetorical strategies central to feminist rhetorics that are associated with rhetorical empathy. They are: "[y]ielding to an Other by sharing and listening to personal stories, [c]onsidering motives behind speech acts and actions, [e]ngaging in reflection and self-critique, [and] [a]ddressing difference, power, and embodiment" (63). Addams' and Fernandes' rhetorical strategies reveal rhetorical empathy in action as both women attempted to connect people across ethnic and socioeconomic lines. Addams, a wealthy white woman, gave up her privilege to work alongside poor immigrant families in Chicago's Hull House and shared their stories in a speech on women's labor rights at an exhibition attended by those women's employers. A century later, Fernandes, a dark-skinned Black woman and the daughter of a domestic worker who also performed that work before she went to college to become a teacher, started a Facebook account that featured stories of Black women who worked in the homes of lighter-skinned women where they faced ridicule and abuse. Fernandes used these stories and her persona as a popular rapper in Brazil to persuade privileged women to see domestic workers as full humans deserving of dignity and rights. Though separated by time, space, and digital technologies, Addams and Fernandes use the same empathy-evoking rhetorical strategies to persuade those in power to change themselves.

Chapter three, "Rhetorical Empathy in the Gay-Rights/Religious Divide," foregrounds rhetorical exchanges among evangelical Christians and gay-rights activist Justin Lee, also an evangelical Christian. In this chapter, rhetorical empathy accounts for the emotional aspects of empathy in bridging divides between progressives and fundamentalists, who can be changed when an abstract Other becomes a concrete Other through storytelling. Blankenship chose this issue because it remains a controversial matter of civil rights most staunchly opposed by evangelical Christians even though a majority of LGBTQ people self-identify as Christian, and because our students often come from one or more of these backgrounds. Blankenship analyzes the features of rhetorical empathy in a blog post called "Ask a Gay Christian" and the rhetorical exchange between Lee (its author) and evangelical Christians in the comments. Lee strategically leverages his antigay, Southern Baptist background to rehearse a devout line of thinking shared by his audience and promote identification with him. When he makes himself vulnerable by sharing painful experiences of rejection, Lee invites his audience to feel that pain alongside him. Disarmed by his vulnerability and identifying with his Christian background, his audience became open to changing their beliefs about gay rights and Christianity. Lee's practice of rhetorical empathy opened space for his interlocutors to become vulnerable to change and growth.

In chapter four, "Beyond 'Common Ground': Rhetorical Empathy in Composition Pedagogies," Blankenship turns to the composition classroom in her locale of Baruch College at The City University of New York. Rhetorical empathy contributes to composition studies by 1) resituating the role of personal writing in composition, and 2) reconsidering typical approaches to teaching argument and persuasion. Drawing on a range of recent composition scholarship, Blankenship reiterates that students find writing projects meaningful when those projects connect to their personal lives, and students are more persuaded by personal stories than logical arguments detached from the body, though this agonistic Aristotelian approach still prevails in popular writing textbooks. Hence, Blankenship advocates for teaching narrative argument, a combination of the personal and the political that connects students' stories to communities. Such a move requires teachers to value the personal as a valid epistemology and form of evidence in research-based academic writing.

I admit to bringing skepticism of personal narratives to *Changing the Subject*, but Blankenship's argument and my students' responses to it changed my perspective. Not only is her students' writing more interesting when they build new knowledge with personal stories, Blankenship notes, but this blending of narrative and argument also attunes her to the realities of her students' lived experiences and affects every aspect of her pedagogy (115). Blankenship continually puts herself in her students' position as novice or near-novice academic writers composing multimodal arguments and, when she can, she does assignments along with them. As a result, she relates to her students differently, more fruitfully.

When my students read *Changing the Subject* in a senior seminar, they said they wanted to re-read this academic book (a first for them) because, when they returned home, practicing rhetorical empathy would help them find their way to their loved ones across profound differences. They hungered for an effective, ethical response to polarized politics, and Blankenship named what they knew but lacked vocabulary to express. Rhetorical empathy resonated with their daily struggles to communicate across differences, and they expressed interest in Blankenship's narrative argument as a more engaging and meaningful form of academic writing. Their experience suggests that teachers are not the only ones who will find *Changing the Subject* illuminating in dark times.

Like any theory or praxis, rhetorical empathy has its limitations and Blankenship discusses them in the epilogue ("Epilogue: A Theory of Rhetorical Empathy"). Rhetorical empathy is but one strategy among many, and sometimes anger, refusal, silence, or disruption is a more fitting choice. If it is not done sincerely, rhetorical empathy can seem artificial, and sometimes people "literally cannot afford to be vulnerable" (122). Change within a person happens over time, too. Most significantly, rhetorical empathy needs an audience open to listening to others, and some people refuse to take this stance. But rhetorical empathy can be effective when other strategies are not, and as such, it has profound implications for composition.

Pocatello, Idaho

The Archive as Classroom: Pedagogical Approaches to the Digital Archive of Literacy Narratives, edited by Kathryn Comer, Michael Harker, and Ben McCorkle. Computers and Composition Digital Press/Utah State UP, 2019. https://ccdigitalpress.org/book/archive-as-classroom.

Reviewed by Moira Connelly, Pellissippi State Community College

Launched in 2008, the Digital Archive of Literacy Narratives (DALN) is an online collection of over 7000 stories of literacy experiences, containing submissions from around the world in text and multimodal formats. Teaching with the DALN in college and university courses, mainly first year composition, is the focus of *The Archive as Classroom: Pedagogical Approaches to the Digital Archive of Literacy Narratives*, an open access, edited collection. Each chapter, preceded by a helpful abstract, offers description, theory, and context for the practical classroom materials housed in the robust appendices, which provide a concrete idea of the instructional context.

Given that the DALN is a collection of literacy narratives, it is not surprising that most chapters focus on literacy narrative assignments. Many perspectives on literacy narratives are presented, but several commonalities arise. First, authors praise the DALN as a source for students to find authentic literacy narrative models, or "mentor texts." The real-life, often student-written texts of the DALN, many authors state or imply, may more accurately reflect the messy and sometimes challenging literacy experiences of a wide range of U.S. college students than the canonical, polished, "literacy-as-success" (Alexander 611) narratives of such writers as Sandra Cisneros, Amy Tan, and Malcolm X. Second, many authors invoke the expanded definition of literacy promoted by the New London Group. Third, multi-modality reigns. Like the texts in the DALN, assignments in the collection call for the use of audio, video, text, or a combination of formats. As a result, authors note a need to help students learn the technical skills necessary to navigate the DALN and to produce the artifacts required for assignments. Many authors begin their students' DALN exposure by assigning a scavenger hunt or orientation activity that gets students searching the database based on personal interest or assignment requirements. To produce the final artifacts for literacy narrative assignments, several authors note that they provide in-class workshop days where students can receive help on the technical skills needed to produce a digital literacy narrative.

The editors offer two digital pathways through the material. The first is organized around the core concepts of the DALN—digital, archive, literacy, and narrative. The second is thematic, grouping chapters by such concepts as curation, reflection, faculty development, inclusion, research methods, rhetorical analysis, and multiliteracies. This review follows the first pathway.

Composition Studies 48.3 (2020): 151–154

The digital section explores the affordances of a digital platform as a medium for presenting and creating multimodal texts. It begins with Lynn Reid and Nicole Hancock's presentation of DALN-based assignments to counter what they see as a still-common skills acquisition approach to Basic Writing. Reid asks her community college students to search the DALN for texts that speak to them, while Hancock assigns students at her small liberal arts university DALN-based assignments to gain digital literacy and research skills. The second and third chapters in the Digital section discuss DALN classroom projects implemented with multilingual students. Janelle Newman and Mary Helen O'Connor argue that interacting with the DALN helps multilingual students to become digitally literate, learn multimodal composing skills, and gain confidence in themselves as students. O'Connor notes that creating a digital literacy narrative allows her refugee students to preserve their personal stories, the only part of their history they may still have.

The Archive section of the collection embraces the notion of an "archival turn" in writing studies that calls for a reconsideration of the value of archives in student research and learning. Cynthia Selfe and H. Lewis Ulman discuss their multi-year project in which students work with members of Columbus, Ohio's African America community to create video literacy narratives to contribute to the DALN. Students then create their own video literacy narratives and write reflective papers on the difference between being behind and in front of the camera. In her piece, Joanna Schmertz argues that online classrooms are themselves a form of archive because the contents and interaction of the course are documented in the learning management system. Her students contribute to the DALN by creating iterative literacy narratives from different perspectives and after engaging with various texts. Deborah Kuzawa argues that the DALN is a queer space because it is pushes the boundaries of the binary constraints of an archive—"restriction/openness, impersonalness/ personless, expert-direction/ self-direction"—to question how an archive should look, what it should contain, and who should control, create, and access it.

The Literacy section examines the types of literacy that engagement with the DALN can promote. Erin Kathleen Bahl focuses on expanding students' religious literacy by having them research a narrative on the DALN about a religious tradition different than their own. Students then "remediate" the narrative in a media form different than the one in which the original narrative is produced, such as audio into video, or alpha into audio. The goal of remediation, Bahl states—as opposed to remixing—is to stay true to the content of the original narrative rather than using it to create a new argument. Kara Poe Alexander notes that writing studies as a discipline seems to offer undergraduates few opportunities to conduct discipline-related research. She theorizes an assignment sequence that would allow undergraduates to expand their archival literacy skills through research in the DALN. Stacey Stanfield Anderson calls for use of the DALN to help students expand their scientific literacy to better judge the veracity of claims and to promote critical thinking and civic action. Like Anderson, Alice Myatt and Guy Krueger use the DALN to provide "mentor texts," or models, for student writing. Their premise, however, is that the DALN can provide mentor texts for genres beyond literacy narratives, such as poetry, argument and reflection.

In the first chapter of the Narrative section, Lilian W. Mina's goal is to help multilingual students improve their reflective writing, which Mina calls "an advanced form of literacy." To do this, she asks students to write their own literacy narratives after analyzing texts by multilingual writers in the DALN. J. Joseph Rodríguez uses the DALN to help in his work with undergraduate pre-service secondary English teachers. Additionally, Christian Smith asks students to remix items from the DALN with their own voices and stories, as well as other open access resources, to produce a "convolute," an audio-visual literacy collage. Smith hopes that students will critique the genre of the literacy narrative with its typical linear structure and "successful" literacy trope.

Because instructors need to document student learning outcomes, it is helpful that several authors explicitly state what students learn from creating literacy narratives and interacting with the DALN. Selfe and Ulman note that students learn interviewing skills, digital media recording and editing, transcribing and captioning, using primary sources, and cataloging items in a public digital archive. O'Connor echoes Selfe and Ulman's learning outcomes of becoming familiar with digital technology and primary sources, and adds that students will practice traditional learning outcomes for first year composition as well, such as writing mechanics and writing process. Additionally, O'Connor believes that engaging with the DALN provides an opportunity for instructors to engage in a discussion about copyright and publication ethics. Selfe and Ulman argue that by working with the DALN, students learn to value oral history and archival preservation. Schmertz notes that literacy narratives allow students to "become conscious of the connection between storytelling and identity-formation."

Although the collection at times feel repetitive because it focuses only on literacy narrative assignments, its strength is the many options to use the DALN, a rich, open access resource that could replace or supplement a course text. In fact, incorporating the DALN into a course could be a straight-forward way to update literacy narrative assignments. Writing this review at time when, because of a pandemic, many of us have been forced abruptly to teach online, I am aware that basing course assignments on a free, easily-accessed resource such as the DALN could benefit students and instructors. An additional open access resource that might supplement DALN assignments is Melanie Gagich's

"An Introduction to and Strategies for Multimodal Composing," in the third volume of the open access textbook *Writing Spaces: Readings about Writing*. Gagich's overview of terms and introduction to the New London Group might be a useful complement to many of the assignments in this collection. Finally, as mentioned above, many instructors do rely on in-person instruction to help students acquire the technical skills necessary to produce multimodal texts. Some of the appendices in the collection reference online videos to explain technology, but it seems that the creation of a digital artifact may still rely to some extent on in-person instruction to make it happen.

Knoxville, Tennessee

Works Cited

Alexander, Kara Poe. "Successes, Victims, and Prodigies: 'Master' and 'Little' Cultural Narratives in the Literacy Narrative Genre." *College Composition and Communication* vol. 62, no. 4, 2011, pp. 608-633.

Digital Archive of Literacy Narratives. The Ohio State University and Georgia State University, thedaln.org/#/home.

Gagich, Melanie. "An Introduction to and Strategies for Multimodal Composing." *Writing Spaces: Readings on Writing*, vol. 3, 2020. https://writingspaces.org/sites/default/files/1gagich-introduction-strategies-multimodal-composing.pdf

Understanding the Paragraph and Paragraphing, by Iain McGee. Equinox, 2018. 438 pp.

Reviewed by Mike Duncan, University of Houston-Downtown

Iain McGee's book about paragraphs is seminal. Here's why.

Everyone who teaches writing reckons with the paragraph eventually. But a comprehensive monograph on the paragraph has never emerged, probably because the task was not a small one. Such a book would need to present the English paragraph from all the myriad angles that scholars have used since Joseph Angus and Alexander Bain and present a unified theory that encompasses most of the paragraph's textual complexity. A few dissertations have attempted to ascend that Everest, notably Edwin Lewis's in the nineteenth century, but McGee is the first to reach the summit.

If you have questions about how paragraphs function or how to treat them in your pedagogy, a handbook or Google might be your first recourse. But I would encourage that this book should be your first stop instead. McGee's complex and descriptivist conclusions will not make the average composition instructor giddy with relief after having glimpsed something of the ultimate, but teaching writing is never a simple matter, and if you think paragraphs are a trivial side concern on the road to successful writing, McGee might dissuade you.

In a perfect world, *Understanding the Paragraph and Paragraphing* would have been written in the late 1980s, just as interest in the paragraph along with sentence combining and the usual grammatical suspects in composition waned, and ideology and cultural studies waxed. If McGee is secretly a time traveler from that period, I recommend he go straight back, as composition studies could have used thirty years with this book available to maintain a stronger connection to its roots as a discipline that struggled (often futilely) with fundamental questions about linguistic structure.

McGee's first two chapters orientate. Chapter 1 offers a clear, reader-friendly overview of the chief theoretical and pedagogical issues that sets up mysteries to be unpacked in later chapters and makes clear that defining the paragraph and sorting through its myriad and reinforcing rhetorical and linguistic functions is no simple task. The paragraph can be viewed as a discourse marker, a highlighting technique, a structural device, a unit of cohesion, an aid to readability, a crutch for developing writers, a pedagogical problem, or all these and more.

Chapter 2 is a historical view of the origins of the paragraph concept, a badly needed update to Lewis's 1894 dissertation that engages and critiques his work directly. McGee begins with the Greek *paragraphos*, a punctuation mark with different functions, including text division, referencing, an aid to oral delivery, and rhetorical emphasis, and traces it forward to its modern English equivalent, using many sources unavailable to Lewis's more narrow justification of Bain's pedagogically simplified paragraph. The ancient and medieval usages of the concept are shown just as flexible and complex as modern ones, forming a strong counterpoint to Chapter 3, which explores what McGee calls the "Era of Terminology," the myriad 19th century attempts to codify and simplify paragraph structure and function. In this timeframe, the paragraph is narrowed down by Alexander Bain and his many imitators into a curious system of rules and topic sentences, governed by an abstract triad of unity, emphasis, and coherence, all more suitable for mass writing instruction. McGee also notes competing germinal ideas about the importance of the reader and paragraph purpose that appear in Chapter 4's post-1960s theory, where more complex ideas about how paragraphs function (and should function) were debated. This history has been told before, but McGee's account has the advantage of a far broader command of how related fields like linguistics, education, and psychology can work together with composition to form a holistic view of the paragraph.

The next three chapters illustrate this depth: Chapter 5 regards the paragraph as a discourse marker, Chapter 6 explores linguistic cohesion, and Chapter 7 centers on psychological aspects of the paragraph, with each chapter synthesizing a broad array of disparate studies from many subfields. For example, McGee notes how different paragraphing styles can manipulate the reader experience; the placement (or omission) of a topic sentence, a shift in indentation, or a match between style and the background knowledge of the reader can create different outcomes in comprehension, retention, and learning. McGee is not sanguine about every avenue, however; he critiques the long history of textual segmentation studies, where previous paragraphs are re-assembled by test subjects to study paragraph formation, holding that they do not factor in the experience of the reader enough.

Chapter 8 marks a formal shift to pedagogy, which is threaded informally though the previous chapters. McGee notes a longstanding pressing need for empirical research, as why writers paragraph the way they do remains poorly understood, and none of the existing models, prescriptive, functional, linguistic, or otherwise, reflect all of the complexities of how writer decides, consciously or unconsciously, to compose and frame their sentences inside paragraphs.

McGee's answer to this challenge in Chapter 9, "Wrapping Up The Paragraph," centers on how the paragraph has so many interconnected aspects – genre, linguistic and extralinguistic context, purpose, context, reading psychology – that only a perspective that encompasses all of these can explain why and how a given paragraph functions, and how facility with these aspects can be taught most effectively. Such a holistic perspective is only partially available, however, due to a lack of empirical work in corpus and computational linguistics, the effects of technology and psychology, and genre variances.

A reader new to this area might be distressed to find a theoretical Olympus Mons lurking behind the Everest that McGee just climbed. But McGee is wise to espouse humility. Understanding the paragraph, as the book is titled, is the task that lies ahead, not a state reachable by reading a single book. Olympus Mons, the solar system's highest mountain, is a good way to think of McGee's paragraph – so vast in profile that it cannot be seen in its entirety from either its summit or any given point on Mars, and even a satellite in orbit cannot really give its scale justice. The book's comprehensive bibliography reflects the work of a scholar who has thoroughly scoured the extensive literature on paragraphs, forming a holistic picture for another generation of scholars that may be intrigued by an over-twenty-kilometer-high shield volcano.

The goal of composition theory, in my view, is to offer teachers of composition the deepest possible understanding of all the nuances of the writing process, so that they can then use that knowledge to teach students to the greatest extent possible. As the concept of the paragraph sits, arguably, at the center of the compositional act, it represents one of the most tantalizing and direct routes to that goal. But unlocking the paragraph proved too much for many a theorist and practitioner. Christenson and Rodgers felt they were close, and Bain and his imitators a century before thought they had it in hand, but the paragraph still rests just outside of our understanding, a strange combination of deceptively simple and limitlessly complex. McGee's book reminds us that the paragraph remains a mystery left unsolved not because it is unimportant, but because the initial explorations offered no quick or easy or convenient answers to the difficult task of teaching composition, and the writing field moved on to ideological and professional concerns that were critical and important but not necessarily exclusive.

In *Understanding the Paragraph and Paragraphing*, McGee offers a multidisciplinary path to the intense study of a central structural aspect of teaching writing. It is also an invitation to take up the quest again. Reading McGee's book has inspired me to return to that path after a long absence. Olympus Mons awaits.

Houston, Texas

Toward Translingual Realities in Composition: (Re)Working Local Language Representations and Practices, by Nancy Bou Ayash. UP of Colorado, 2019. 254 pp.

Reviewed by Demet Yigitbilek, Illinois State University

A highly addressed topic in the field of composition and applied linguistics (Canagarajah; Horner et al. Motha et al.), translingualism and translingual literacy, Canagarajah states, look at the understanding of production, circulation, and reception of texts that are always mobile, drawing from diverse languages, symbol systems, and modalities of communication that involve inter-community negotiations ("Negotiating Translingual Literacy"). To add to these conversations, Nancy Bou Ayash's recent book, *Toward Translingual Realities in Composition: (Re)Working Local Language Representations and Practices,* aims "to make visible the dynamic negotiations of language-ideological tensions ... to develop a richly textured and more useful translingual understanding of language and composition ... by advancing the translingual paradigm in superdiverse literate contexts" (xi-xiii). To do so, she approaches the "conflicting yet co-existing language ideologies and their unique and complex negotiations"—both in the U.S. (Seattle) and outside (Beirut)—and the teaching of academic writing in these contexts for the primary audience of writing researchers, teachers, and administrators (6).

Ayash studies young writers from two cities that she defines as superdiverse, linguistically and socio-culturally, and presents both the differences and unexpected similarities through her five-year transnational ethnographic research. In doing so, she acknowledges her multiple positionality and intersecting roles as a writer, researcher, teacher, transnational individual, and activist in taking on the complex task of addressing the diverse manifestations of various language ideologies in sometimes conflicting sociolinguistic realities and their material effects.

In the introduction, Ayash details the terminology she will use in the book, a much-appreciated and needed strategy for such a broad topic. She gives her rationale for terms like superdiverse ("as a cover term more tuned to the complexity, unpredictability, and messiness of the dynamics of language and cultural difference"), monolingualism, multilingualism, translingualism, and postmonolingualism, and pays respect to all the scholars who have coined and expanded their uses (13).

Chapter one, "Language Ideologies in Teaching Writing: A Language Representations and/as Practices Perspective," details dominant and conflicting language ideologies: monolingualism; multilingualism, an alternative yet "a surrogate to monolingualism" (42); and translingualism, a counterhegemonic approach to how language(s) are represented to show how ideologies impact our language-related activities. Starting with excerpts from three cases where the instructors show their ideologies in the way they respond to moments of language difference in students' writing, Ayash identifies key features, limitations, and affordances of these three orientations fully; this is a very helpful strategy not just for novices in the field but for experts, as well, to fill the gaps in understanding.

Chapter two, "Working Translingual Language Representations and/as Practices," draws from sociolinguistics, and Ayash highlights the fluid and mobile nature of language. She urges readers to pause and look at the concrete practices in which language users engage and the possibilities translingual approaches can offer. To make the complexities and reality of language use clearer, she presents three metaphors—the rhizomatic banyan tree, moving traffic, and a chaotic arrangement of overhead electricity cables models—to describe transdirectionality and transcentricity as well as transversality of networks of sociocultural and historical meanings of interpretive possibilities (50).

Following such grounding theorizations, in chapter three, "Unpacking Local Language Representations and/as Practices: Portraits of Postmonolingual Tensions from Beirut," Ayash gives a detailed description of sociolinguistics in the educational context of current-day Beirut, and in chapter four, of Seattle. She examines how students in such seemingly different contexts negotiate their writings in accordance with the complex and dynamic sociocultural, linguistic, and educational situations. Her analysis of the local contexts in these chapters demonstrates how young writers in her study engage in multiple language representations—which at times conflict with their identities and desires based mostly on the local networks at play—causing them to (re) negotiate their orientations towards language in diverse interactions in daily life and educational settings.

After presenting clear, detailed pictures of the cityscapes of Beirut and Seattle, in chapter five, "Translingual Activism: Turning up the Volume of Critical Translation in Writing Pedagogy," Ayash forges an activist path with translation as an analytical tool for meaning-making. She sheds light on the activism that translingualism affords for writing instruction in deliberate and strategic ways and explores its possibilities and challenges. Detailing her ongoing project on translation as re-writing, Ayash invites writing teacher-researchers to collaborate in creating a bridge by moving away from the traditional and limited ways of defining translation practice toward practices that enable not only multilingual students but also monolinguals to view language as dynamic, fluid, and negotiable—all of which are key points in understanding translingualism. The course design she shares, with her assignment prompts and student responses, gives a detailed picture of how this strategy can benefit many students in first year writing by extending the practical implications of a translingual approach that so far has been highly insufficient. To this end, her critical and practical approach to translingualism in composition classrooms presents a replicable implementation of a highly valued but underrepresented ideology in practice. The book concludes with observational insights presented as building blocks for expanding a) our understanding of translingualism ideology in language and b) language diversity as embodied literate practices influenced directly by a complex network of contextual features.

Ayash sets a solid ground for her arguments in the entirety of the book through detailed descriptions and expansions of key terminology and ideologies that influence how we view language and diverse language practices. Her research in two local contexts presents how these language ideologies are enacted in so many (super)diverse ways due to various complex networks. Ayash also shows her stance clearly and expands on the work of many scholars: applied linguists, sociolinguists, and compositionists. In doing so, her work highlights how deeply English monolingualism is rooted not only in U.S. composition classrooms but also in different parts of the world where English is used and taught as a foreign or second language. Her research also clearly demonstrates the heterogeneity of language users who can seem so similar yet show a huge degree of variety in the way they view language and language difference in different rhetorical contexts. Through a translingual approach and translation as a writing strategy used in her activism, she also exemplifies how translingual ideology can be taken up and used in predominantly monolingual classrooms. Although the course design she forwards in chapter five may not be so easily implemented in any first year writing classroom in the US—her study took place in two superdiverse cities—it still provides readers with a much-needed practical example and resource to increase student awareness on diverse linguistic practices and empower them to express themselves by focusing on their agency and creativity.

Lastly, her suggested pedagogical practices are invaluable for furthering the scholarship in translingualism in writing studies. This book serves as significant in challenging the long-held Standard Written English monolingualism and therefore can be taught in graduate level courses in English departments and with undergraduate students who are prospective teachers working with a diverse body of students in US contexts.

Normal, Illinois

Works Cited

Canagarajah, Suresh A., editor. *Literacy as Translingual Practice: Between Communities and Classrooms*. Routledge, 2013.

Canagarajah, Suresh. "Negotiating Translingual Literacy: An Enactment." *Research in the Teaching of English*, vol. 48, no. 1, 2013, pp 40–67.

Horner, Bruce, et al. "Language Difference in Writing: Toward a Translingual Approach." *College English,* vol. 73, no. 3, 2011, pp. 303–21.

Motha, Suhanthie, et al. "Translinguistic Identity-as-Pedagogy: Implications for Teacher Education." *International Journal of Innovation in English Language Teaching and Research,* vol. 1, no. 1, 2012, pp. 13–28.

Contributors

Jennifer Ansley is faculty in the Thompson Writing Program at Duke University. Their scholarship in Writing Studies and Queer Studies is concerned with practices and discourses of care and caregiving. Their scholarly and creative non-fiction work has appeared in *New England Quarterly, Abusable Past, Scalawag Magazine*, and *Crab Fat Magazine*.

Bruce Bowles Jr. is Assistant Professor of English and the Director of the University Writing Center at Texas A&M University–Central Texas. His research interests focus on how we evaluate and make judgments across multiple contexts, including writing assessment, writing center administration, and political and public discourse.

Christina V. Cedillo is Assistant Professor of Writing and Rhetoric at the University of Houston-Clear Lake. Her research examines embodied rhetorics and rhetorics of embodiment at the intersections of race, gender, and disability. Currently, she is co-chair of the CCCC Latinx Caucus and Committee on Disability Issues in College Composition.

Moira A. Connelly is Associate Professor of English at Pellissippi State Community College in Knoxville, Tennessee. She has published in *Teaching English in the Two-Year College*. Her current research interests include writing transfer, assessing the writing of multilingual students, and writer perceptions of inclusion in collaborative writing.

Vanessa Cozza is Career-Track Associate Professor in English at Washington State University, Tri-Cities. She teaches writing and advanced rhetoric courses and supervises her department's internships. Her scholarship focuses on implementing client-based projects into the classroom by creating opportunities for students to collaborate with and learn from local professionals.

Joshua Cruz is Assistant Professor of qualitative research in the College of Education at Texas Tech University. His research interests include high-school-to-college transitions, innovations in qualitative methods, academic writing, and occasionally Brazilian martial arts.

Mike Duncan is Professor of English at the University of Houston-Downtown.

Jim Fredal is Associate Professor of English at the Ohio State University working in classical rhetoric, rhetorical history and theory, legal rhetoric, the enthymeme, rhetorical inference, and argumentation studies. His recent book, *The Enthymeme: Syllogism, Reason, Narrative* is available from Penn State University Press (2020).

Laura Hardin Marshall is a doctoral candidate in Rhetoric and Composition at Saint Louis University. Her research focuses on the intersection of response and revision, specifically how writing instructors and consultants respond to students and how students in turn use that feedback in their revision processes.

Asao B. Inoue is Professor and Associate Dean of Academic Affairs, Equity, and Inclusion for the College of Integrative Sciences and Arts at Arizona State University. He was the 2019 Chair of CCCC. His many articles, chapters, and books on antiracist writing assessment have won numerous awards.

Ashanka Kumari is Assistant Professor of English at Texas A&M University–Commerce where she teaches undergraduate and graduate courses in writing and rhetoric. Her work has appeared in *Kairos: A Journal of Rhetoric, Technology, and Pedagogy*; *Composition Studies*; *WPA: Writing Program Administration*; and *The Journal of Popular Culture*, among others.

Paul Lynch is Associate Professor of English at St. Louis University.

Elizabeth Maffetone is a Visiting Lecturer at Indiana University, where she also worked as a tutor and writing program administrator. Her research focuses on rhetorical violence in pre-modern texts and modern pedagogy.

Talitha May is an artist and researcher living in Portland, Oregon—the City of Roses.

Rachel McCabe is Assistant Professor and Director of Writing at La Salle University. Her scholarship has been published in *Textshop Experiments* and *Research in Online Literacy Education* and is forthcoming in *Pedagogy*. Her research focuses on the affective experience of reading and viewing texts and how doing so impacts the student writing process.

Rachel Morgan is the author of the chapbook, *Honey & Blood, Blood & Honey* (Final Thursday Press, 2017), and she is the Poetry Editor for the *North American Review*. Currently, she teaches creative writing and composition at the University of Northern Iowa, where she also co-coordinates a first year writing program.

Mya Poe is Associate Professor of English and Director of the Writing Program at Northeastern University. Her books include *Learning to Communicate in Science and Engineering, Race and Writing Assessment*, and *Writing,*

Assessment, Social Justice, and Opportunity to Learn. She is series co-editor of the Oxford Brief Guides to Writing in the Disciplines.

Patricia Roberts-Miller is Professor Emerita of the Department of Rhetoric and Writing at the University of Texas at Austin and is the author of several books, including the forthcoming *Speaking of Race: Constructive Conversations about an Explosive Topic* (The Experiment).

Brita M. Thielen is a doctoral candidate in English with a concentration in Writing History and Theory at Case Western Reserve University. Her current research examines how writers construct textual identity and ethos in food writing texts, particularly in the cookbook, food memoir, and food blog genres. Additional interests include intersections of identity, social privilege, and equity in the writing classroom.

Jamie White-Farnham is Associate Professor in the Writing Program at University of Wisconsin–Superior, where she has taught first year and major courses. Her work, published in *Rhetoric Review, College English, Computers and Composition*, and others, focuses on rhetoric, activism, and writing program administration.

Lydia Wilkes is Assistant Professor of English and former writing program administrator at Idaho State University. She has published in *Composition Forum, The Journal of Veterans Studies*, and *The Proceedings of the Annual Computers and Writing Conference*, 2016-2017.

Demet Yigitbilek is a PhD student in English Studies at Illinois State University where she designs and teaches FYC. Her research interests center around translingualism and linguistic diversity in Applied Linguistics and Composition. So far, she has taught FYC as Language and Identity, Critical Writer-Researchers, and Composing In/Of Our Lives.

Deb Dimond Young teaches first year integrated communication and composition at the University of Northern Iowa and is currently working on a PhD in rhetoric and professional communication at Iowa State University. Her research interests include composition pedagogy, community-engaged writing, and feminist rhetoric.

PARLOR PRESS
EQUIPMENT FOR LIVING

NEW RELEASES

The Art of Public Writing by Zachary Michael Jack

A Genre Analysis of Social Change: Uptake of the Housing-First Solution to Homelessness in Canada by Diana Wegner

The Naylor Report on Undergraduate Research in Writing Studies edited by Dominic DelliCarpini, Jenn Fishman, and Jane Greer

Internationalizing the Writing Center: A Guide for Developing a Multilingual Writing Center by Noreen Lape

Socrates at Verse and Other Philosophical Poems by Christopher Norris

Writing Spaces: Readings on Writing Volume 3 edited by Dana Driscoll, Mary Stewart, and Matthew Vetter

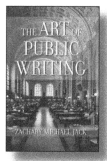

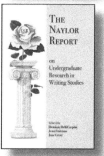

FORTHCOMING

Collaborative Writing Playbook: An Instructor's Guide to Designing Writing Projects for Student Teams by Joe Moses and Jason Tham

CHECK OUT OUR NEW WEBSITE!

Discounts, open access titles, instant ebook downloads, and more.

And new series:

Comics and Graphic Narratives. Series Editors: Sergio Figueiredo, Jason Helms, and Anastasia Salter

Inkshed: Writing Studies in Canada. Series Editors: Heather Graves and Roger Graves

www.parlorpress.com

CPSIA information can be obtained
at www.ICGtesting.com
Printed in the USA
BVHW031510221220
596060BV00005B/13

9 781643 172088